*The Unity
of the
Platonic Dialogue*

THE LIBRARY OF LIBERAL ARTS

The Library of Liberal Arts

PUBLISHED BY

The Bobbs-Merrill Company, Inc.

INDIANAPOLIS · NEW YORK

RUDOLPH H. WEINGARTNER

The Unity
of the
Platonic Dialogue

THE CRATYLUS
THE PROTAGORAS
THE PARMENIDES

For Fannia

Acknowledgments

Quite a few people have taken the trouble to read earlier versions of various parts of this book and have given me the benefit of their comments and suggestions. I am indebted to all the members of the Vassar philosophy department for their help —especially to Professors George Berger and Michael McCarthy —as well as to Professors John L. Ackrill of Oxford University, Arthur K. Bierman of San Francisco State College, Eric Havelock of Yale University, David Keyt of the University of Washington, and David Savan of the University of Toronto. I am grateful to the editor of *Phronesis* and to its publisher, Royal Vangorcum Ltd., Assen, The Netherlands, for permission to use here, as the first chapter, an expanded version of "Making Sense of the *Cratylus*," which first appeared in that journal (Vol. 15, 1970).

I owe great thanks to Professor Gregory Vlastos of Princeton University, not only because he took the time to read drafts of all three chapters of the book and let me have the benefit of his comments, but because his kind encouragement helped me to overcome the sort of doubts that must beset anyone who works on an author as complex and as extensively discussed as Plato. Above all, I was always aided by the light Professor Vlastos' own papers shed on the writings of Plato and by their very existence as models of philosophical scholarship.

During all the stages of writing this book I shamelessly exploited Professor James Day of the Vassar classics department. I called on him often and he unstintingly made available to me his great knowledge of the Greek language, of which my own grasp is feeble indeed. I am grateful, too, to Miss Constance Wardrop, who diligently undertook the labor of locating in the Greek text the exact lines of the many quotations used here and to Miss Lindsay Scampole for research on the characters of the *Protogoras*. None of these kind helpers is, however, responsible for the views expressed in this book nor for any errors that may be found therein.

Mrs. Norma Mausolf was burdened with the job of typing several versions of many parts of the book, in addition to the final copy. Her cheerful efficiency and unerring accuracy made my work immeasurably easier.

The Unity of the Platonic Dialogue is dedicated to my wife, Fannia, whose experienced editorial eye scrutinized its every line. My debt to her, however, transcends her role as editor and goes far beyond the limits appropriate to an acknowledgment page.

SEPTEMBER 1971   R. H. W.

Contents

Introduction

I

Philosophy in the West began with thinkers who addressed their audience in maxims, aphorisms, or verse. Socrates compelled his audience to join him in conversation, while Plato—except for a few letters—wrote dialogues. Then came Aristotle; through his writings, the professorial manner was impressed upon philosophy, so that readers of works in that domain soon became accustomed to a fare of treatises and essays. Today, we are so strongly habituated to prosaic disquisitions that we tend to be uneasy when confronted with deviations from that norm.

Plato wrote dialogues. Many of those who have commented on him have expressed their perplexity at not finding philosophy wrapped in a familiar package by essentially ignoring that fact. Obeisance is paid to form, at least in the case of the more dramatic dialogues, by introductory remarks concerning Plato's desire to present philosophy as it is lived; but for at least two types of Plato interpreters, the substance of his philosophizing remains unaffected by what is considered its literary dress.

The first of these—and I want to sketch out *types* of approaches to Plato, not give an historical account of Plato scholarship—takes Plato to be putting forward a doctrine. The dominant participant in each dialogue—most frequently Socrates or the Eleatic Stranger—is held to speak for Plato himself. These leading characters, according to this view, make their primary contribution not to the specific dialogue in which their words are recorded, but to a Platonic doctrine which lies outside any given work. To be sure, the continuity of the exposition is broken up by questions and objections that are interjected by the other participants in the conversation; but these interruptions are seen as mere literary devices which provide Plato's prolocutor with plausible opportunities for stating and clarifying his views. They also perform a function similar to that of the objections with which Thomas Aquinas begins each article of the *Summa Theologica:* as a means of paying heed to other men's opinions and as a convenient foil for his own exposition.

There are at least two species of this—call it the doctrinal—approach to Plato. Some readers see a nontemporal Plato standing behind and above the temporal sequence of his dialogues. For them, Plato's spokesmen expose in piecemeal fashion different components of a single philosophic system. Others see Plato's doctrine as undergoing change and his deputies as contributing to a developing position. Both types of interpretation, moreover, may insist on a special treatment of the earliest Socratic dialogues, where these may be held not to be Platonic, but reasonably accurate accounts of the views of Plato's teacher. Whatever the variations, however, the distinctive mark of this approach to Plato's work is the dual assumption that some personages in his dialogues are merely masks for their creator and that the words they speak may be removed from their dialogic context and then conjoined to make up a continuous exposition of the Platonic doctrine.

The second way of ignoring the fact that Plato wrote dialogues is to use his works as a rich mine of philosophic ore. Plato's writings contain a myriad of arguments and concepts, an abundance of suggestive metaphors and heuristic similes, numerous myths pregnant with meaning, and sundry analyses that illuminate a great variety of philosophic problems. The dialogues hold within them, futhermore, the basic principles of diverse philosophic positions, as well as depictions of the kinds of persons who adhere to them. It is thus not surprising that so rich a source should tempt many generations of philosophers to use Plato for their own purposes.

Needless to say, those who help themselves to one or another piece of Plato and put it to use in their own philosophizing tend to pay little attention to the fact that this building material was originally presented in dialogue form. They want
to press into service the idea of Socrates as gadfly or of Thra-
symachus as moral cynic, the conception of the philosopher-
ruler or the image of the psyche as a charioteer with his two
horses, the notion of the forms as exemplars or the conception
of being as immutable. Whether these and other Platonic in-
ventions are merely mentioned in passing or whether they are
elaborately worked out, they are apt to be treated as if they
were ripe fruit scattered on the ground of some philosophical
Garden of Eden. They are there to be consumed and no attention need be paid to the labor that produced them.

But even among those whose interest in Plato is more
scholarly, there are many who treat his works as if they constituted a mine. Particular arguments, conceptions, or myths, as
well as passages that contain more or less elaborated philosophic principles, are detached from their contexts and subjected to detailed scrutiny. That Plato wrote dialogues is more
often than not ignored: the words are taken as if they were
asserted by their author; no attention is paid to the fact that
they are spoken by one of the characters of his creation.

The enterprise of mining Plato for the purposes of one's
own philosophizing is made worthwhile by the fertility of
Plato's philosophic imagination; similarly, the complexity and
inventiveness of his writing and the intrinsic interest of what
he says make this piecemeal scholarly approach to Plato a
rewarding experience. Nor is there any question that much
illumination has been shed on Plato's work by such close scrutiny of particular texts. It is not always noted, however, that
this approach has serious limitations. Plato wrote dialogues.
The dramatic context of a particular argument or speech may
have an important bearing on its meaning; to consider a
speech or argument in isolation—however interesting it may
be when taken up for its own sake—may not lead to an under-

standing of what the dialogue actually says. And because Plato wrote dramatic works, the whole is greater than the sum of its parts. It therefore cannot be taken for granted that when interpretations of isolated passages are placed side by side, the result will be an understanding of a Platonic dialogue as a whole.

Not all writers on Plato have ignored the fact that he wrote dialogues. On the contrary, some make the dramatic nature of his works the central fact in their understanding of Plato. Except in his few letters (which are addressed to specific individuals or small groups), Plato never speaks to the reader in his own person; the entire body of his work consists of conversations of which he is the sole author, but never a participant. This singular fact has led interpreters of Plato to claim that he is much more correctly likened to a playwright than to Aristotle and to other professors of philosophy.

The view that Plato is essentially a dramatist, moreover, is often linked to a particular understanding of the nature of a dramatic work. Only the playwright's fictional creatures make assertions; the author says nothing for himself. The artist possesses "negative capability" and holds no opinions of his own: instead, he is "capable of being in uncertainties, mysteries, doubts, without any irritable reaching after fact and reason."[1] Hamlet, at one point in his dramatic career, declaims that "conscience does make cowards of us all and thus the native hue of resolution is sicklied o'er with the pale cast of thought." No such belief, however, can be attributed to Shakespeare, who placed these words in Hamlet's mouth. The playwright exhibits the world of Elsinore in all its complexity, but even though his medium is language, he *says* nothing at all; he only *shows*.

---

1. *Letters of John Keats,* selected by Frederick Page (London: Oxford University Press, 1954), Letter 32, p. 53. Whether this conventional interpretation of the passage is an adequate one is another matter.

Thus, when Plato's dialogues are read as dramatic works, they are often regarded as rich depictions of the philosophic life. What is stressed is process, ongoing inquiry, and the interactions among the created personages of the dialogues. The earlier works, particularly, are looked upon as *tranches de vie philosophique,* in which the *character* of Socrates plays the leading role and the primary concern is with his attitude toward life and the way it conflicts with the attitudes of the various interlocutors he engages in discussion. If this is the nature of the picture Plato is thought to be painting, then the precise formulations of the questions that are asked and the exact way in which the arguments are propounded appear to affect it only minimally. Accordingly, those readers who take the dramatic character of the dialogues most seriously often take least seriously the details of the text Plato wrote.

In one sense, the later dialogues are not so easily regarded as slices of the philosophic life. They are much less dramatic in that Plato uses fewer and fewer stage directions, makes less and less effort to characterize the participants in a dialogue, and, above all, adopts the practice of writing a significant role for only a single character. Nevertheless, even in these works, Plato has been held to be primarily an artist and man of negative capability. He is seen as refraining from asserting positions of his own *throughout* his life—at least in his dialogues. At all times, he is regarded as putting forth what are, at most, *possible* views and *possible* solutions to problems, but as never committing himself to anything. Even where genuine conclusions seem to be reached by persons in his dialogues, they must not be attributed to Plato.

Once again, the way in which Plato's dialogues are assessed affects the way in which they are interpreted. Even in the late works, more stress is likely to be placed on process than on outcome, on question than on answer, on arguing than on argument. If the author of the dialogues himself is considered to be showing primarily what philosophizing is like and to be abstaining from making assertions, his interpreters are easily led to follow in his footsteps, by not attaching full seriousness to what Plato's dialogic creatures say.

Plato wrote dramatic works; but he was not a man of negative capability. Plato *does* speak to his readers through his dialogues; they are not adequately understood unless the scholarly approach of detailed textual examination is combined with the insights of those who see Plato as remaining in some ways aloof from what he has his characters say. No doubt the form in which he addresses his audience shows that Plato has at least as great an interest in thinking as in thought; no doubt the dialogue is used by him to exhibit philosophy as an activity that human beings engage in. But the undeniable significance of this aspect of Plato's work is no reason for ignoring precisely what Plato's characters say or for omitting to ask just why Plato has them follow the script he wrote for them.

Plato wrote dialogues: a mind—one that is not identical with the minds of Socrates, the Stranger, Parmenides, Callicles, Protagoras, Meno, and all the rest—composed each of the works, and for a purpose that is not the same as the purposes displayed by these characters. Plato is not reduced to choosing between showing and saying: a dialogue may have a theme—even a conclusion—which is Plato's and not that of his creatures, a theme which is upheld by the entire work, although it may never be explicitly stated within it.

No evidence can be given for such a claim about the Platonic dialogues in general; support must come from the detailed examination of particular works. We know that a particular dialogue fulfills a specific purpose of its author when it can be shown to do so. And to demonstrate such a fact—if it is one—calls for far more than a statement of what is taken to be the dialogue's leading motif. The theme of a Platonic dialogue is extrinsic to it only in the sense that it is not stated as such by one of the participants in the discussion; in a vital, though different, sense it is an all-pervasive feature of the work. Evidence that Plato was conveying specific philosophic themes by means of his dialogues must take the form of showing how, on the one hand, that theme unifies the work and renders it a whole and, on the other, how it makes intelligible its component parts—speeches, arguments, characterizations—in relation to each other.

II

In this book, I take three dialogues—the *Cratylus,* the *Protagoras,* and the *Parmenides*—and attempt to show, in some detail, that each of them can—and therefore should—be understood as a unified whole. The dialogues discussed differ considerably from each other, as do the themes which serve as their principles of unification. On the one hand, this dissimilarity should make whatever success I may have in exhibiting the philosophic-dramatic structure of each of these dialogues all the more convincing support of my general thesis about the unity of Platonic dialogues; but on the other hand, the fact that our dialogues differ so from one another requires that each be dealt with in a somewhat different fashion.

The *Cratylus,* to which the first chapter is devoted, is simple in form and straightforward in execution. Three characters—Socrates, Hermogenes, and Cratylus—are engaged in a discussion about language. There is no narrator; they simply talk. Socrates discusses the difficult subject of the true nature of names, first with Hermogenes, then with the more formidable Cratylus. And although the dialogue ends with Socrates' insistence that true knowledge is not to be found merely by examining names, no positive conclusion appears to be reached concerning the question discussed in the main portion of the work.

Looked at in one way, there is no fundamental problem of interpretation, no puzzle about the dialogue's unity. Plato can be regarded as being immensely skillful in composing a philosophic conversation with all the marks of verisimilitude. The participants in the discussion are familiar types; we still encounter them frequently. Hermogenes, a reasonable fellow, makes no claim to expertise, although, like most of us, he does have some sort of opinion about language. Cratylus, on the other hand, has studied and has come to firm conclusions, which he is ready to assert dogmatically. Socrates, as he does so often, quizzes both of them and finds that neither of their views can stand up to analysis. The topic is a difficult one, in which definitive conclusions are hard to come by. The conversation of the three is thus "realistic," even to the point of including arguments that are not quite right and a long and rambling—and in part humorous—digression. This is how people do talk when they meet casually, especially if one of them is Socrates.

And yet, this way of looking at the *Cratylus* leaves a great deal unexplained. Why does Plato take up the particular theories about names which he has Hermogenes and Cratylus propound? How are we to understand the theory Socrates begins to propose, especially since it closely resembles one which that same Socrates demolishes with much vehemence? Is the etymology section a mere *jeu d'esprit,* or does this kind of assessment not justify *anything* that Plato might have had his characters say? The slice-of-philosophic-life interpretation of the *Cratylus* is unsatisfactory, not merely because it does not answer questions such as these, but because it does not even ask them.

In the first chapter, I attempt to show that the *Cratylus* has a philosophic theme of considerable importance to Plato's thought. Hermogenes and Cratylus maintain theories of naming which, were they sound, would make dialectic impossible. Plato's aim is to keep the way clear for dialectic inquiry. An understanding of this theme of the dialogue as a whole enables one, as well, to answer the kinds of questions raised in the previous paragraph and to show how the work's various parts become intelligible, not simply as isolated arguments or speeches, but as functioning components of a unified work.

The *Protagoras,* to which the long second chapter is devoted, is artistically a much more complex dialogue. To begin with, it is narrated by Socrates so that, in addition to an account of the words that are spoken in the discussion, we have descriptions of persons, their actions, and their surroundings. Instead of three characters, we have many—among them well-known persons, including three famous teachers, in addition to Socrates. The conversation itself is lively and varied; the forward propulsion of the dialogue is impressive.

Plato displays an unquestioned mastery here in presenting a full-scale double portrait of a much respected, elderly Protagoras and of a critical and argumentative Socrates. Their discussion takes the form of a duel fought before an audience; Protagoras propounds his views and Socrates exposes their weaknesses. Two of Plato's predecessors are thus skillfully depicted: their views, their philosophic styles, their attitudes, and mannerisms.

But is Plato actually painting portraits of historical figures and, if so, is he doing no more than that? No satisfactory answer can be given to the first of these questions. We have too little information about Socrates and Protagoras beyond what Plato himself supplies to be able to check Plato's pictures against their originals by means of historical research; we thus have no way of assuring ourselves of the accuracy of his depictions. Just the same, one might insist that the dialogue is intrinsically convincing and hold that its portraits do resemble their originals—on the assumption that Plato would not have falsified his portrayals for a contemporary audience that *did* have independent knowledge of Socrates and Protagoras. Nevertheless, this question must be asked: precisely just how much of Plato, in the *Protagoras,* is historian and how much philosopher-artist?

It is no doubt plausible to maintain that Socrates and Protagoras believed and behaved, in a general way, as Plato's characters do; but surely what Plato writes in the dialogue is not *exactly* what they did and said on some particular occasion. But there *is* that dialogue; it says specific words were uttered and specific gestures made on a particular morning. The existence of those words and gestures can be accounted for only by reference to the author of the dialogue in his role as philosopher-artist; it is too incredible to suppose that the *Protagoras* is the product of a historian who reported, as best he could, just what had been seen and heard.

Once again we must interpret the various components of the dialogue as fulfilling an *author's* purpose, a purpose that goes far beyond recording what might in fact have happened. If the Socrates in the *Protagoras* argues fallaciously, we must find out why Plato has him do so and why Plato has Socrates propound the particular arguments we find in the text. If Protagoras loses his temper, it is not enough to say that the great Sophist was irascible; it must be determined why Plato has him become angry just when he does. When, at the end of the dialogue, the two main disputants appear to have changed positions and Socrates admits to being much confused, we must ask whether *Plato* took his protagonists to have switched sides and whether the author of the *Protagoras* is confused as well.

The dialogue is a complex one; numerous questions of this sort can be posed. In the second chapter of this book I attempt to answer such questions (without actually formulating them first as questions) by giving a detailed account of the entire dialogue. I do so in the light of a thesis about the work as a whole. Plato pits two conceptions of morality and education against each other and shows, by means of a dramatic interchange between Socrates and Protagoras, that the very problems the Sophist aims to solve require the philosophic methods and commitments of Plato's Socrates. The many components of the dialogue can, in this way, be seen as constituting a unified work.

The dialogue discussed in the last chapter is markedly different from the previous two. Although the *Parmenides* is narrated, only its opening passage makes use of the possibilities this technique affords. The rest proceeds, without relief, to pile unadorned argument upon argument. While one might regard the *Parmenides* as a realistic depiction of a pair of philosophers hard at work, no one is likely to be tempted to find a principle of unity in this fact. On the other hand, if one seeks a unifying principle in its philosophic substance, one is immediately confronted by a number of serious obstacles.

The *Parmenides* consists of two very dissimilar parts. In the first and shorter one, Parmenides and the young Socrates discuss the theory of forms, while in the second, Parmenides—with a youthful Aristoteles as the monosyllabic respondent—delivers himself of a long exercise in dialectic. It is difficult to see these two sections as parts of a single whole.

Even Part I of the *Parmenides* taken alone is seldom seen as having genuine inner coherence. The entire passage, to be sure, consists of critical arguments which Parmenides directs against the theory of forms. But why do these arguments belong together? What is the outcome of this effort by the father of Eleatic philosophy? The dialogue does not contain a defense of the forms by Socrates, nor do either of the interlocutors suggest that the forms should be abandoned. Furthermore, while some of Parmenides' arguments appear to be sound, others clearly are not; and the validity of the most interesting one of all is much disputed. What, then, is Plato doing in the *Parmenides?*

I try, in the final chapter, to show that the *Parmenides* as a whole performs a complex task to which all its parts contribute. Plato is here engaged in revising his views on *both* the method by which knowledge is attained and on the nature of the objects of knowledge themselves. This principle not only holds together the two major parts of the dialogue, but

serves as a key, as well, to the puzzle of the first section. In
the larger part of the chapter on the *Parmenides* I propose
to show that if the arguments Parmenides makes against the
forms are taken *cumulatively,* that is, in relation to one another and to the purpose of the entire series, a good deal of
the mystery that has surrounded them disappears.

That the *Protagoras* is a "dramatic" dialogue is obvious.
It is a grave mistake, however, to identify drama with elabo-
ration of setting, stage directions, characterization, and entertaining language. While the *Parmenides* lacks just about
all these, it is dramatic nonetheless. The drama of a Platonic
dialogue can be concentrated entirely in its arguments, as
it is in the first part of the *Parmenides*. Each argument has
a conclusion that is explicitly stated; but taken together, they
have a significance that goes beyond this. They show Plato
in the process of revising his conception of the forms. The
purpose of the whole dialogue illuminates its parts.

III

A final word about procedure. Because in each chapter I attempt to show how a single theme functions in the interpretation of a dialogue's component parts, they all include a
good deal of what might be called interpretative exposition.
As a result, each chapter is likely to be intelligible even to
someone not familiar with the dialogue being discussed, although there is no question that knowledge of it would be
helpful. In any case, I try to supply quotations from the text
wherever my interpretation depends upon the exact words
used by Plato; at all times, I refer the reader to the passages
discussed.

As much as possible, the focus of each chapter is confined
to the dialogue under discussion. With an author such as Plato,
however, this cannot mean that everything else may sensibly
be omitted. The secondary literature on the Platonic dialogues

is immense; and while I cannot pretend even to have looked at large parts of it, I have by no means ignored it. On many occasions, I readily accept the assistance which Plato scholarship—especially that of recent decades—offers to someone who is attempting to understand Plato's works, while in other cases I find it useful to disagree explicitly with someone else's reading of a passage. But in order to realize, as expeditiously as possible, the aim of seeing a Platonic dialogue as a whole, I have, with some exceptions, relegated polemical exchanges with fellow readers of Plato, past and present, to the realm of footnotes.

Nor can Plato's other dialogues be completely ignored when any particular one is under discussion, although there is no simple criterion for deciding where they should be brought in. Plato, the philosopher, is not born anew in each work composed by him. While his interests and views may have changed in the course of a long career, it is nonetheless the same mind that produced all the dialogues. It is important to see this and to see it in concrete terms, although it does not follow that in the discussion of a particular work, one should take note of and comment on every echo stemming from other works of Plato.

Purely rhetorical reasons account for the introduction, in these chapters, of *some* references to other works. With their aid, it is often possible to illuminate more clearly and economically a particular passage that is being explicated. In other instances, however, my commentary goes beyond the dialogue under discussion for somewhat weightier reasons. Plato did not begin at the beginning in each of his works. Although the dialogue form has no room in it for footnotes directing the reader to the author's previous writings, it nevertheless permits the author to convey that what he is saying calls for knowledge that is to be gained from other works. The reader of a Platonic dialogue must thus be sensitive to the cues Plato weaves into his compositions and must pursue them. Accordingly, I look for assistance, at times and for specific reasons, to works that may be assumed to have been written earlier than the dialogue in question.

On still other occasions, it may be possible to illuminate a given work by placing it in a context that includes writings that were composed *after* it. Philosophers are not always clear in their own minds what they are about, but in time may become more sure-footed as they work out their insights. In the case of Plato, too, some of his earlier passages may be rendered more intelligible by considering them from the perspective of the philosopher's later reflections. This holds particularly for an understanding of what Plato says about the forms.

Scholarly literature on Plato, references to earlier works by Plato, references to later writings—these are all means, at best, to the understanding of specific dialogues. In the chapters that follow, the focus, finally, is on particular works. I now take up, in turn, the *Cratylus,* the *Protagoras,* and the *Parmenides.*

1

The Cratylus and the Defense of Dialectic

I. Introduction

Too many readers of the *Cratylus* have looked upon this dialogue as a series of ill-connected passages in which Plato takes up a number of problems about language and, above all, presents "a picture of Socrates in one of his more whimsical moods."[1] In addition, commentators have found the *Cratylus* to be a useful mine for bits and pieces of information on topics which Plato takes up elsewhere, particularly the theory of forms and the Heracleitean flux. No doubt the character of Socrates *is* depicted in the *Cratylus* in a vivid way; and no doubt we do learn about Plato's thoughts on language and other topics from a reading of this work. But neither this particular portrait of Socrates engaged in discussion nor the reflections on the nature of names can be adequately understood without a grasp of the structure of the *Cratylus* as a whole.

And the *Cratylus* is a whole—a unified work held together by a single overriding purpose. In this chapter, I wish to offer an interpretation of the *Cratylus* which makes manifest this

---

1. A. E. Taylor, *Plato: The Man and His Work* (New York: Meridian reprint of the 6th ed., 1956), p. 78. The entire sentence reads: "The real purpose of the dialogue, so far as it has any purpose beyond the preservation of a picture of Socrates in one of his more whimsical moods, is to consider not the *origin* of language, but its use and functions."

unity and philosophic aim and which looks at the various parts
of the dialogue in the light of that totality. First I shall briefly
summarize what Plato is doing in the *Cratylus* and then begin
at the beginning of the dialogue.

Three theories of names are taken up in the *Cratylus*—
that of Hermogenes, that of Cratylus, and the one which
Socrates himself begins to develop. The two by Socrates' part-
ners in discussion are refuted by him and the reason for his
doing so is crucial: if either Hermogenes or Cratylus were correct, the method of dialectic as a road to the achievement of
knowledge would be impossible. The search for knowledge requires language as an indispensable means. Hermogenes' peculiar conventionalism and Cratylus' representational view of
names make it impossible to utilize this instrument, whereas
Socrates' own position on the nature of names is especially well
suited to the task of philosophy. Cratylus' doctrine, however,
goes beyond language; thus, because Cratylus holds names to
be the very objects of knowledge, Plato has his Socrates conclude the dialogue with a brief excursion into some larger
questions.

Nevertheless, the central problem of the *Cratylus* is that of
naming, taken up not for its own sake but in relation to the
Platonic conception of the method of philosophy. Once this
philosophic purpose of the *Cratylus* is clear, there is no difficulty in seeing the dialogue as a unified composition.[2]

II. HERMOGENES (383a–385a)

The dialogue has no narrator; it simply opens as Hermogenes
and Cratylus, who have been "arguing about names"

---

2. It may be useful if I state here how I divide this dialogue:
   383a–385a: Introduction and statement of Hermogenes' position
   385b–390d: Refutation of Hermogenes; development of Socrates' view
   390d–427d: Transitional passage and section on etymologies
   427d–438e: Transitional passage and the refutation of Cratylus
   439a–440e: Coda on the conditions for knowledge.

(383a4–5),[3] invite Socrates to join them. Socrates is willing and testifies to the importance of the topic; but he also makes clear that he does not know the truth about such questions as the correctness of names. Poverty had prevented him from taking Prodicus' fifty-drachma course on language; the one-drachma course which he did audit was not enough.[4] Nevertheless, he invites the disputants to state their positions and Hermogenes begins.

"I . . . cannot convince myself that there is any principle of correctness in names other than convention and agreement" (384c9–d2); this first statement by Hermogenes of his views is quite correctly labeled a "conventionalist" theory of naming, but it is not the one Hermogenes comes to hold nor is it the position actually attacked by Socrates. Hermogenes goes on: "any name which you give, in my opinion, is the right one, and if you change that and give another, the new name is as good as the old" (384d2–4). But just *who* does the name-giving here is not so clear. It could be the community, so that language would indeed be a matter of convention—of coming together—but it might also be any given individual at any given time. In the exchange that immediately follows this pronouncement, the ambiguity is resolved. Hermogenes agrees that Socrates could rightly use the name "horse" to refer to a man, while at the same time the rest of the world (also rightly) refers to men by the name "man." This is the view which Socrates then sets out to refute; and to call *it* "conventionalism," as is sometimes done,[5] is misleading in the extreme. The meaning of "convention" would already be stretched beyond the breaking point, I think, if it referred to a consistent use of names by only a single individual, for we should then have to say that

---

3. Unless otherwise indicated, the passages cited are in the revised Jowett translation: B. Jowett (trans.), *The Dialogues of Plato* (4th ed., rev.; Oxford: Clarendon Press, 1953), III, 41–106. This translation is cited by permission of The Clarendon Press.

4. For a protrait of Prodicus, see the *Protagoras,* especially 315c–316a. See also Ch. 2, Sec. II, 3.

5. For an example, see Jowett's introduction, *Dialogues,* III, 3.

he comes together with himself (con-venes) and enters into agreements with himself. But when, as is implied by Hermogenes' statement of his view, even an individual user of a language may, without being in error, employ different sounds at different times to designate the very same object, we no longer have convention or agreement in any sense whatever.

Hermogenes is confused and no doubt Plato wishes to exhibit the confusion of so bright and pleasant a young man. Hermogenes has not accepted the views with which Cratylus had harangued him before the opening of the dialogue, but neither is he clear as to just what view he does hold. Plato is interested not only in contending against the doctrines of his professional predecessors and contemporaries such as Heracleitus, Parmenides, Protagoras, and others, but in showing up the inadequacy of Athenian practices of education. He does this by depicting the muddledness of its most intelligent and well-meaning products: Glaucon and Adeimantus, who, in the *Republic,* are capable only of giving arguments for a position which is the opposite of the one they hold; Hippocrates, who is eager to study with Protagoras but has no idea what he might thus be learning;[6] and Hermogenes here.

Under Socrates' questioning, Hermogenes' view, with its sensible reference to a conventional aspect of language, quickly becomes so deformed that it hardly qualifies as a view of language at all. For we might note that this Humpty Dumpty position fails to take into account a central function of language: the communication of thoughts by one person to others. Unless the sounds that are used as names have a fairly stable relationship to the objects they are meant to denote, this cannot be accomplished. Thus, if Hermogenes were right, there could not be any such activity as dialectic.

This entailment becomes obvious after a moment's reflection on the nature of dialectic. "How real existence is to be studied is, I suspect, beyond you and me" (439b4–5), says

---

6. See Ch. 2, Sec. II, 2.

Socrates, but he is not reduced to utter silence on the subject. In the first place, Socrates has a position on what is to be known. At the very end of the *Cratylus,* in the coda on the conditions for knowledge, he insists that this "real existence," the object of knowledge, must be abiding, rather than subject to change, "for no knowledge, I assume, can know that which is known to have no state" (440e2–4). Thus, whatever account of naming may be correct, names themselves cannot be the ultimate objects of knowledge, since they are but sounds or inscriptions[7] and thus subject to the vicissitudes of the Heracleitean flux.[8]

Nor, secondly, is Socrates completely ignorant about the means by which "real existence is to be studied or discovered." To be sure, he does not know enough about the method to be able to show how following it would lead by successive steps to certain knowledge. Indeed, Plato probably never thought that a method which guaranteed success could be devised at all.[9] For success means understanding; and the most a method can contribute to that goal is to put things in such a way that they *can* be understood. A method, then, is a more or less refined procedure for pointing; and between pointing and seeing there is a gap that cannot be bridged by following a rule.[10] But if Socrates had to be ignorant about how to *succeed* in obtaining knowledge, Plato was not silent on the subject of how to try. In the first place, there is no Platonic dialogue, the *Cratylus*

---

7. Gilbert Ryle argues that in the *Cratylus,* names thought of as *sounds* are at the center of the discussion, rather than names as written. But as far as the issue here is concerned, the distinction does not matter. See his "Letters and Syllables in Plato," *Philosophical Review,* 69 (1960), 431–451.

8. This does not merely follow from the facts that all objects of the senses are in flux and that sounds or marks in stone or on papyrus are objects of hearing and seeing; it is also established more directly in the course of Socrates' examination of various etymologies. At times, Socrates comes close to "true opinion" about the empirical development of language. See Sec. V.

9. See the discussion in Richard Robinson, *Plato's Earlier Dialectic* (2nd ed.; Oxford: Clarendon Press, 1953), pp. 72–74.

10. See especially, *Republic* 532–534.

included, which is not an exhibition of such an attempt. And secondly, there are numerous dialogues in which Plato makes the method of philosophy the subject of discussion.[11]

Common to any evidence that might be cited on the subject of what dialectic is and common to all the conceptions that Plato may have had throughout his long career is the fact that dialectic consists of talk. For Plato, one does not seek knowledge by going into a trance or by interpreting dreams or omens; nor does the method of knowledge call for the manipulation of nature in measurement and experimentation. Dialectic, rather, is a way of thinking, and language is its vehicle. The means to knowledge of a nonlinguistic reality, therefore, is language.

If this is not enough to show that Hermogenes' position, if it were true, would make dialectic—and hence the pursuit of truth—impossible, more can still be said. The very meaning of "dialectic" tells us something about the conditions under which it must be carried on, for it is "the power of conversing," "the art concerning discussion," "the procedure of discussions."[12] It consists of the methodic organization of questions and answers, of the proposing of hypotheses and of their examination, of a sorting out of types of objects by means of concepts, using what is later called the method of collection and division. Throughout, dialectic is a way of *conversing;* it is a communal mode of inquiry. The philosopher is not thought of as thinking quietly in retreat from his fellow men.[13]

---

11. The clearest examples of these, however, are works likely to have been written later than the *Cratylus,* e.g., the *Phaedo, Republic, Phaedrus, Sophist,* and *Statesman.* There is agreement that the *Cratylus* was written before the *Republic,* but it has been argued that the interval between them was small. See David Ross, *Plato's Theory of Ideas* (Oxford: Clarendon Press, 1951), pp. 1–10, and J. V. Luce, "The Date of the 'Cratylus,' " *American Journal of Philology,* 85 (1964), 136–154.

12. Robinson, *Plato's Earlier Dialectic,* p. 69.

13. See the discussion in Robinson, *ibid.,* pp. 75–84. Numerous references to Plato's works are given there, but note particularly the defense of conversation against the claims of writing in *Phaedrus* 274–278.

Only one philosopher is needed to be ruler of a city, but a society of philosophers is required if any one of them is to be a philosopher. And above all, there is Plato's choice of the dialogue form. The entire body of Platonic writings is a monumental demonstration of the fact that however much the possession of truth may be a grasping by a particular mind of what is the case, the road that leads to this achievement must be traveled in the company of others.

There is thus no need to settle the question whether for Plato or for anyone else there can be such a thing as a private language, nor need one agree that the view Hermogenes comes to hold is incompatible with the possibility of a private language—just in case there is such a thing. If there is to be dialectic, its communal character makes it eminently necessary that Hermogenes be refuted.[14]

III. Cratylus (427d–438e)

The bulk of the dialogue (385b–427d) lies between this brief statement of Hermogenes' unconventional conventionalism and the discussion of Cratylus' own position; but I now want to turn to this second view of naming which, if it were true, would make dialectic impossible. Cratylus holds that names are natural signs, that they are so constituted that they reflect, imitate, or represent that to which they refer. This much we have known all along; Hermogenes reports it to Socrates at the very opening of the dialogue. In that same passage (383a–b), however, Hermogenes also complains that Cratylus has not made clear just what he means and that he remains mysterious and oracular. A good part of Socrates' refutation of Cratylus consists of an attempt to dispel the mystery and to get clear

---

14. Because the refutation of Hermogenes is so very closely tied to the exposition of Socrates' own view, I shall attend to it only when I get to Socrates in Sec. IV.

about the relation between names and what is named. In this way the passage resembles the first part of the *Parmenides*,[15] though the shoe here is on the other foot.

What Cratylus says is hard enough to grasp. A name reveals the nature of the thing named; in order to refer and thus be a name, a sound must tell us what the thing it refers to is like. But it cannot do so more or less well: the relationship between name and thing named is not analogous to that between a portrait and the subject painted, where the painter can produce a greater or lesser likeness of his model. If the sound that is made in the attempt to name an object deviates in the slightest from what it ought to be, it is not a poorly fashioned name, but nonsense (429e). Whatever in any way falls short of perfection in the representation of the intended referent does not refer at all and is thus not a name. Instead, the putative name is but "an unmeaning sound like the noise of hammering at a brazen pot" (430a4–5).

It can readily be shown that this position is no less disastrous for dialectic than is Hermogenes'. Begin by supposing (in contrast to what Cratylus gives us) that we understand in just what way names indicate the natures of the things they name; let us assume that we know just how different sounds imitate or represent characteristics of every kind. There are then three possibilities for our language, for the sounds that we actually use in the naming we do or at least intend to do. First, all these sounds may indeed measure up to Cratylus' strict standard, so that as long as we know the language we are speaking, every attempt at naming succeeds. Second, it may be that no word in our language satisfies the criteria of Cratylus' representationalism, so that we never refer to anything at all. And finally (and this seems to be Cratylus' own view of the matter), our language might contain some sounds that do and some that do not fulfill the requirements Cratylus places upon names.

---

15. To which the better part of Ch. 3 is devoted.

Next, let us attempt a philosophic inquiry that is completely typical of Plato's dialectical procedure, whether one thinks of the early Socratic dialogues or of a late one such as the *Statesman*. We begin by asking "what is justice?" in the hope that extensive analysis in conversation will at least bring us closer to knowing what justice is. According to Cratylus' view of naming, however, what have we done? If our language is in good shape, or at least if the part we have just used is, the question that was asked contains the answer. If "justice" names, then it already shows us the nature of what it names: in asking what it is, we have already referred to the properties it has. Accordingly, the first sentence of our dialectical inquiry must also be the last. If, on the other hand, our language is not a natural one in Cratylus' sense, or at least not the portion of it that is being employed, we have not asked anything at all. "What is justice?" is equivalent to saying "what is BANG?," where the reader must imagine the striking of a brazen pot. According to this pessimistic view of the state of our language, the first "sentence" of our inquiry will also have to be the last —this time, however, because it is not an intelligible question at all and hence cannot be answered.

While the question of the form "what is *x*?" is the most typical beginning of a philosophical inquiry, the difficulty just pointed out is not the only way in which Cratylus' theory of naming makes dialectic impossible. A good part of dialectical discussion is devoted to the examination of some claim: that justice is helping your friends and harming your enemies, for example, or that the virtues are essentially one. But how would Cratylus' view permit our investigating such a hypothesis? How could careful examination lead either to progressive improvements of the thesis put forward or to its ultimate abandonment? *Either* the statement is true *or* it is nonsense. If it is true, then we have completed our job before we have begun; if it is nonsense, there *is* no hypothesis, no claim to examine, hence nothing that could slowly be revealed to be untenable. If we have spoken nonsense, we must sit in silence until, like a philosopher's oracle, we are ready to spew forth all at once the whole truth and nothing but the truth. Everything that is dialectic or any sort of inquiry has been short-circuited by the requirement placed upon naming.

It may seem obvious that a condition for dialectic is the possibility of making statements that are true; but it is not at all sure that Plato's conception of the road to knowledge requires this. Yet while at first it may not be so clear that the nature of philosophic inquiry demands that we can say things that are false, there is no doubt that the possibility of falsehood is an indispensable condition for the method of dialectic. In the dialogue, Cratylus' view of language is only briefly stated. However, little reflection is required to see that if it were correct, dialectic would be impossible. For we should then have to say either what is true or we should have to utter nonsense; but we could not say what is false.

Each of the points that Socrates fires off at Cratylus in quick succession is made succinctly and is fatal. Three times Socrates focuses on the way in which words are alleged to represent what they name. In his first effort (430d–431e)[16] to make sense of this relation, he attempts to make an analogy with the art of painting. Cratylus, however, rejects it: while a painting may represent its subject more or less well, "the case of language, you see, is different" (431e9–10), we are told.

Having failed to make the naming relationship intelligible by means of this analogy, Socrates next proceeds to a powerful argument (432a–433c) which undermines, on logical grounds, the very possibility of *perfect* representation, regardless of what the mode of representation might turn out to be. This is the ingenious argument of the two Cratyluses: a perfect representation of Cratylus in all his characteristics would not be a representation at all, but a second Cratylus. Hence a com-

---

16. I make these divisions somewhat arbitrarily at those points at which Cratylus reasserts his position, even in the face of the arguments made against him.

pletely natural language without any element of convention
is logically impossible.

The major point of the third passage (433d–435d) is of a
more empirical sort; indeed the evidence for it had already
been presented in the passage on etymologies.[17] Suppose we
agree on some scheme according to which the elements of
names—sounds as represented by letters—are said to express
various characteristics of things. While, in general, the way for
this has also been prepared by the long middle section of the
dialogue, it is now brought out explicitly that actual names do
not necessarily represent the things named in conformance
with this more or less natural code. In different Greek dialects,
different though similar names are used to refer to the same
thing; letters are inserted that have no place according to the
strict criteria of imitative naming. At the heart of the word for
hardness (*sklêrotês*), for example, stands the letter *lambda*,
which, it is agreed, is the chief representation of softness. And
yet, in spite of many such deviations from the requirements of
representational naming, *we understand:* "the word is intelligible to both of us; when I say *sklêros* (hard), you know
what I mean" (434e1–3). Custom, convention—Socrates is
quite explicit on this point—play their role in naming and account for the fact that we can communicate with each other
(434e–435d). (Socrates' insistence here on convention should
be recognized as a confirmation of the fact that, unless we are
prepared to say that Socrates flatly contradicts himself, his
opposition to Hermogenes' position is not an attack on any
conventional conventionalism.)

The final two points against Cratylus take up the problem
of how knowledge might be gained from a consideration of
names. First (435d–437d), according to Cratylus, information
about things is given us by names: "I believe that to be both
the only and the best sort of information about them," says
Cratylus, "there can be no other" (436a1–2). How much this

---

17. See Sec. V, where the etymology section is discussed.

doctrine differs from Plato's need hardly be explained; the coda already referred to emphasizes that the objects of knowledge must not be in a Heracleitean flux and thus cannot consist of language. For the time being, however, Socrates is satisfied to point out some quasi-empirical difficulties with Cratylus' reliance upon names. We have no assurance, to begin with, that the original giver of names did a good job: if we try to learn about things from existing names we may well learn no more than the mistakes made by the name-giver (436b–d). Moreover, the long string of etymologies has already shown that names hardly reflect a consistent metaphysics. According to some of them, the world would seem to be in motion; according to others, at rest (436e–437d). According to Cratylus' account of names, the information they convey would in fact have to be unreliable.

There is a still more serious objection, however (438a–e), one that points to a logical flaw in Cratylus' doctrine. How could names be given at all, especially if they must be "true" ones, if the knowledge of the *things* named does not serve as a standard that is prior to and independent of the names given? Even if we waived all the problems by which Cratylus' account of natural naming is beset, it would still founder on the fact that it presupposes the existence of objects of knowledge that are *not* names. If name-giving can be done correctly, so that it gives information about things above and beyond the names themselves, these things must be objects of knowledge. They must in some way be directly accessible to our minds and not merely through the mediation of names. Language may indeed be a necessary means to knowledge, but it remains only a means. Cratylus' attack on the foundations of dialectic has been successfully parried.

IV. SOCRATES (385b–390d)

We are now ready to consider Socrates' own contribution to the theory of naming, an account that grows immediately out of the refutation of Hermogenes. Recall that for Hermogenes, Humpty Dumpty has the correct view of language: no one name is more correct than any other. When asked, however, Hermogenes acknowledges that we can make true and false statements, that there is a distinction between them. This admission then becomes the basis of a bad argument against Hermogenes which can easily mislead one into believing that what follows is also tainted by the error that is here introduced. The procedure at this point is simplistic and mechanical: if there are true and false statements, then their parts must be respectively true and false as well. Since the smallest parts of statements are names, it follows that names must be either true or false (385b–d).

Nothing is made of this conclusion. Socrates goes right on to place the whole issue into a larger context. Protagoras is brought into the picture and, not surprisingly, Hermogenes confesses that he has been attracted by the dictum that man is the measure of all things (385d–386a). What follows is a refutation of Protagoras' extreme relativism, on the grounds that it is incompatible with the common sense observation that some men are wise or good and others foolish or bad. While this manner of dismissing Protagoreanism has quite rightly been called perfunctory[18]—especially when it is compared with the elaborate consideration of that doctrine in the *Theaetetus*—it is not in itself unsound and does, after all, reappear even in that later full-scale discussion of Protagoras' theory of knowledge.[19]

Now, if Protagoras is wrong "and things are not relative to individuals" (386d8), then "they have some fixed reality of their own" (386d9–e1).[20] And this already very general statement is broadened out still further by Socrates as soon as he

---

18. J. V. Luce, "The Date of the 'Cratylus,' " pp. 146–147.

19. *Theaetetus* 160c–179b.

20. I here prefer H. N. Fowler's translation to Jowett's rather Aristotelian "permanent essences." *Plato: Cratylus, Parmenides, Greater Hippias, Lesser Hippias* ("The Loeb Classical Library" [Cambridge, Mass.: Harvard University Press; London: William Heineman, 1963]), p. 17.

receives Hermogenes' assent. "Does what I am saying apply only to the things themselves, or equally to the actions which proceed from them? Are not actions also a class of being?" (386e6–8). By a circuitous route Socrates not only refutes Hermogenes' doctrine, but reaches the premise he needs for a development of his own view: "actions also are done according to their proper nature and not according to our opinion of them" (387a1–2); and, since "naming is also a sort of action" (387c10), "names ought to be given according to a natural process" (387d4–5) as well. Hermogenes is refuted: we cannot make names any old way.

How this conclusion functions in the development of Socrates' view, however, can occupy us only after a brief reflection on what has happened up to this point. Given Hermogenes' admission that names may be true or false, Socrates could easily have made explicit that his young friend's strange doctrine was untenable, for Socrates' conclusion here is incompatible with the view that any arbitrarily chosen name is the right one. Hermogenes, after all, did not bring up Protagoras; if the refutation of Hermogenes was Socrates' only goal, there was no need for Socrates to make life more difficult for himself by introducing a doctrine which he does not hold anyway. Why, then, does Socrates not claim his victory right at this point (385c)? Why does he bring in Protagoras at all?

The answer to the first of these questions is simple. While I am only reasonably sure that Socrates knew that the argument he was making was bad, I am positive that he considered its conclusion false. Unless it were seriously modified, the claim that all names are either true or false is indistinguishable from Cratylus' position, one which Socrates later destroys with the most powerful arguments of the dialogue. If Socrates had claimed victory over Hermogenes here, he would have been forced to elaborate this most alien conclusion, instead of getting away with merely touching on it fleetingly. If this is correct, an entirely different question must then be raised, namely, why did Socrates assert this position at all? The answer to this, however, must be postponed to the final section of this chapter, for it involves an understanding of the unity of the entire dialogue, which will there be the subject of discussion.

There is a second reason why Socrates does not claim his early victory over Hermogenes and brings in Protagoras, apparently gratuitously. Socrates wants to change the mode in which the subject of the dialogue is discussed. The *Cratylus* begins with a consideration of the truth and falsity of particular *names;* what Socrates now wishes to talk about is the rightness or wrongness of the activity of *naming.* While the truth or falsity of names is under discussion, the most plausible and least complex standard of correctness to which one might appeal consists of the different objects which the names purport to name. Posed in this way, the solution which readily offers itself to the problem of names is some sort of correspondence theory of the truth of names and thus leads one straight into the arms of Cratylus. It will force one to share all the miseries to which that doctrine is subject.

Socrates wants objectivity; he proposes to find it, however, not in the character of the names themselves, but in the activity of naming. The standard of correctness to which he wishes to appeal is that which is generated by the goal that is to be accomplished in the proper giving of names. Thus, Protagoras' grand dictum is a convenient way by which the focus of the dialogue can be shifted. From true and false names we go—at the expense of Protagoras—up to the independent reality of all things and actions and then back down again to the action of naming. A crucial turn in the course of the dialogue has been brought about with great economy of means: instead of the truth or falsity of names, we shall now be discussing correct or incorrect ways of naming. If the shift from names to naming is not seen, the fact that Socrates and Cratylus maintain very different positions can never become clear.

Actions—cutting, burning, weaving—have an independent
nature of their own. If we wish to succeed, they cannot be performed in just any way the whims and desires of particular
actors may dictate. The objective character of the world (the
hardness of things to be cut, for example, the inflammability
of things, the characteristics of yarns) determines the opera-
tions that must be performed, though only if the goals that are
to be accomplished are also posited (shearing off one portion
of a thing from the rest, consuming things by means of fire,
separating the warp from the woof). The goal—what is to be
accomplished, in general or in detail—also serves as the measure of adequacy of the operation. Moreover, all these and
many other actions are performed "with a proper instrument"
(387d5), one that is suitable for the proper performance of the
operation in question (387d–388b).

Thus Socrates prepares the ground for the development of
his own account of naming by drawing upon the characteristics of the familiar crafts—an analogy he maintains throughout his exposition. The exposition itself is brief and schematic
(only two pages remain to be discussed); there are very few
details. Yet precisely because he so clearly treats naming as a
craft, the account of Socrates' view is properly filled out by
means of and within the framework of the craft analogy.[21]

---

21. In what follows I diverge considerably from Richard Robinson's reading of the *Cratylus*. See his "The Theory of Names in Plato's *Cratylus,*" *Re-
vue Internationale de Philosophie,* 9 (1955), 221–236, and "A Criticism of
Plato's *Cratylus,*" *Philosophical Review,* 65 (1956), 324–341. I do not believe,
however, that this difference is the product of different standards of interpretation, with only Robinson living up to the rigorous ones he set down
in the first chapter of his *Plato's Earlier Dialectic,* pp. 1–6. Instead, a good
part of this disagreement can be accounted for by Robinson's erroneous
belief that Socrates' and Cratylus' theories of naming are the same, a
point of view which affects his entire interpretation. It makes the craft
analogy unnecessarily puzzling for him ("A Criticism," pp. 329, 332–333), and
it makes Socrates' indifference to just what sounds a "correct" name is
made up of incomprehensible ("disconcerting") to him ("The Theory," p.
235), to give but two examples. In his second article he speaks of "the
nature-theory of names which Plato made his Socrates develop in the

In discussing the action of naming in more detail, Socrates relies on the specific analogy of weaving. In weaving, the weaver separates the warp from the woof; the instrument by means of which he does this is the shuttle. The shuttle, in turn, is made by the carpenter; but he must make it in such a way that it can perform its function in the process of weaving. We use names "to give information to one another, and to distinguish things according to their natures" (388b10–11). The user of the name (the counterpart of the weaver) is the teacher (388c) or the dialectician "who knows how to ask questions . . . and how to answer them" (390c6–8) and the maker of names (the counterpart of the carpenter who makes the shuttle) is the legislator (388d). But this account is not quite accurate. Socrates is aware that others besides weavers might in fact weave, that others besides carpenters might in fact make shuttles and, certainly, that not all weavers and carpenters need be skilled practitioners of their craft. We all use names, but not every name is the product of the skilled legislator's work: skilled teachers and dialecticians—those who communicate knowledge to others and those who seek it out in the first place[22]—are those who use names *well* and skilled legislators are the expert (but not the only) makers of names.

Over and over again, Socrates insists on *skill,* on doing the job well (388c–e); to note this is of fundamental importance

---

Cratylus, the theory, namely, that 'everything has a right name by nature' " (p. 324), and there quotes words (383a) spoken by Hermogenes about Cratylus' opinions before Socrates has even said a word in the dialogue. This slip, itself of no importance, is symptomatic of the mind-set which never questions the thesis that Socrates and Cratylus hold the same view. Since he never considers the entire dialogue as a *whole,* Robinson fails to notice that the attribution of a single doctrine to both these protagonists renders the work radically incoherent. Even for an adequate understanding of its parts, the dialogue must be seen as a whole.

22. Socrates moves from teacher to dialectician without noting that he has made a change in identifying the skilled user of names. This shifting from one to another counterpart of the weaver reflects the view that teaching and research are not separate activities at all. This is made explicit at 436a.

if one is to understand the theory of naming Socrates proposes. His analysis of how names function in discourse constitues a recommendation as to how they should be made if they are to perform their functions *well*. His theory is not primarily an account of how names are *actually* made, but of how names *ought* to be made. I say "not primarily" not to hedge the point, but because I want to make clear that for Socrates there is no sharp distinction between what is the case and what ought to be; rather, there is a continuum which has at one end the making of names very poorly, so that they are barely names at all, and at the other end the perfect making of names in which the product can perfectly fulfill its function in dialectical discourse. But the very fact that it is possible for us to speak of such a continuum depends upon the conception of an ideal way of making names that will serve as the measure of any and all actual and proposed givings of names.[23] Accordingly, Socrates must be understood as giving an account of how naming should be done, if it is to be a perfect instrument for the enterprise of dialectic.

"To what does the carpenter look in making the shuttle?" (389a6–7). The answer to this crucial question is immediately given: he looks "to the way in which the shuttle must, in the nature of things, operate" (389a7–8).[24] The carpenter, Socrates goes on, does not use as his model some broken shuttle he seeks to replace, but "look[s] to the form according to which he made the other" (389b3), a form which might "justly be called the true or ideal shuttle" (389b5).[25]

The introduction of forms requires a short digression. Until

---

23. Two brief remarks about corroboration. That there is perfect and imperfect name-giving is borne out not only by some of the arguments Socrates makes against Cratylus' position (see Sec. III, above) but by a number of passages in the section on etymologies, to be discussed in Sec. V. That Plato thinks of the crafts and, more generally, of all sorts of activities as being capable of being performed more or less well is shown in more than one dialogue. This conception is worked out and much used in the *Republic*, particularly.

24. ἆρ' οὐ πρὸς τοιοῦτόν τι ὃ ἐπεφύκει κερκίξειν.

25. αὐτὸ ὃ ἔστιν κερκίς.

Plato comes to write the *Parmenides,* he *uses* forms as means
to the solution of various problems with which he is concerned; not until that later dialogue does he reflect upon them.
It is thus misleading to attribute to Plato a *theory* of forms
prior to the *Parmenides*—a theory, that is, so held in mind that
the various characteristics of forms and the implications of the
supposition that they exist are explicitly considered and taken
up for what they are.[26] But in the absence of a theory upon
which one might rely in an attempt to ascertain what Plato has
in mind when he refers to forms, we are forced back to the
context in which he introduces them and to the problem he
there seeks to solve. It therefore pays to examine carefully
what the carpenter is said to look to when he makes a shuttle;
indeed, only in this way can we find out the nature of the
model the legislator employs as he gives names to things.

The form of the shuttle, we saw, is identified with the way
in which the shuttle must by nature operate. Socrates goes on
to emphasize this by insisting that the form which the carpenter embodies must be "naturally most suitable to its special
work" (389b10–c1), where that work is not weaving *simpliciter,* but weaving thin garments or thick, weaving wool or
flax. But not all properties of physical shuttles are possessed
by this shuttle-form which serves the carpenter as model, for
when the maker of shuttles expresses "this natural form, and
not others which he fancies," he does so "in the material, *whatever it may be,* which he employs" (389c4–6), in *"whatever
sort of wood may be used"* (390b1–2). The *function* of the
shuttle, as specified by means of an analysis of the process of
weaving and as that process is seen from the perspective of the
weaver who is intent upon producing a certain kind of product, determines the properties of the form of the shuttle. And
only these properties need and should be considered. Whatever attributes a shuttle has that do *not* affect its functioning
in weaving are not relevant to the nature of that form.

---

26. See Ch. 3, especially Sec. II.

No doubt in the case of shuttles, shape plays a vital functional role, since weaving depends in large part on the shape of the implement that separates warp from woof. Nevertheless, even here "form" does not mean "shape," for a shuttle, if it is to do its job, must also be smooth and rigid and have a certain weight. And when we generalize to other instruments —as Socrates immediately does—the properties a thing must have so that it is "naturally adapted to each work" (389c4) will vary as much as the functions which different instruments are called upon to perform. Form-properties are function-properties.[27]

The legislator proceeds as the carpenter does. Perfect naming requires the legislator to keep an eye on the perfect name of a thing, that which is appropriate to its nature. But let us not be led astray: "we must not misinterpret that different legislators will not use the same syllables" (389d8–e1). Names in different Greek dialects and in foreign languages can all be equally correct, for not the material of which they are made but their function determines their nature. Sounds and syllables are the analogues of the types of wood of which shuttles are made; as such, they are irrelevant to the correctness of the names which they make up. We know from this alone that when Socrates finally turns to it, Cratylus' account of names must be rejected, for that representationalism takes the measure of the correctness of names to be the relationship between the nature of things and the stuff of which their names are made. But here we see that it is the *user* of names who determines their adequacy, and he does so by considering how names must function in the activity in which they play their part as instruments. That user is the dialectician and teacher; his activity is the pursuit and communication of knowledge.

---

27. Whether forms, in the *Cratylus,* are in some sense paradigms or whether they are more like criteria is a separate issue from that just discussed. But see J. V. Luce, "The Theory of Ideas in the 'Cratylus,' " *Phronesis*, 10 (1965), 21–36, in which it is argued that in the *Cratylus* Plato does not conceive of forms as transcendental.

For Socrates, then, the correctness of names is measured by their suitability for the dialectician's work.

This is where Socrates stops, but I should like to continue for another paragraph or so to speculate on what the ideal language hinted at by Socrates is like. To begin with, it is given by the legislator, by a Solon who has unquestioned authority over the entire city and bequeaths his legacy of names to the community. Names are given in the law (388d); they must have the force and acceptance of custom. Hermogenes' extreme view, as we know already, is wrong. But names must do more than communicate; they must help us to "distinguish things according to their natures" (388b10–11). It seems that Plato was here looking forward to a technical language which would reflect the classifications that result when dialectic becomes collection and division, as it is described in the *Phaedrus* and employed in such dialogues as the *Sophist* and the *Statesman*.

Imagine well-nigh complete knowledge of some domain, a theory that indicates the nature of the things belonging to it, one that gives us their definitions. It would then be possible to compose names by choosing syllables to designate different aspects of the nature of the thing named, so that the name in effect constitutes an abbreviation of the definition. Moreover, since the theory puts its definitions into a systematic order, well-made names will show how the things they refer to are related to each other. Nowadays such languages exist: medicine, botany, zoology (to name only a few sciences) have developed sets of names which systematically reflect the organization of the things they name.[28] To a trained scientist the long Latin name of a bug or flower conveys a great deal of information about it and its relation to other insects and plants. What sounds are used in the construction of these names does not matter; historical accident accounts in good part for the

28. See Ronald B. Levinson, "Language and the *Cratylus:* Four Questions," *Review of Metaphysics,* 11, (1957), 37–39, for a similar suggestion.

particular syllables that are used to designate different types or aspects of things. But it is important that the name-giver be a scientist who knows both the objects he is naming in the context of the science that deals with them and the system of syllables that has become the convention in the domain to which his object belongs. It does matter that this system be used consistently, that it be fully accepted by the community of scientists.

That Plato himself did not develop such a technical vocabulary should not surprise us, though he called for one again in his later years.[29] The use of such a language, in the first place, would not have been congenial to Plato in so far as he was a dramatist and poet. Yet more importantly still, he who sets out to reform the language in accordance with the ideal suggested in the *Cratylus* implies that he takes himself to be a legislator, "who of all skilled artisans in the world is the rarest" (389a2–3). He must be the man who knows, the philosopher, in the idiom of the *Republic,* who has had a vision of the forms. But Plato never went so far as to claim this about himself. He gave up poetry, but never the dialogue form. To the end of his life he preferred to suggest, to put forward views to be discussed, examined, and modified. He was never willing to assert that he was in possession of the final truth.

V. THE ETYMOLOGIES AND THE UNITY OF THE DIALOGUE (390d–427d)

At the very beginning of the dialogue Cratylus says "if you please" and then remains silent for forty-four of its fifty-seven (Stephanus) pages. And yet, however the dialogue may have come by its title, the name-giver has acted well. Of the two positions discussed which, if they were true, would render dialectic impossible, that of Cratylus is much the more powerful. Not only is it more plausible than Hermogenes' and, however

---

29. *Sophist* 267d–e.

defective, more carefully worked out than that young man's casual view, but as Robinson points out, it has a peculiar appeal for a Greek rationalist mind that likes to see its universe with all the pieces in place.[30] Moreover, Cratylus' theory of naming is only too readily confused with that of Socrates' own, a confusion of one doctrine that is disastrous for dialectic with another that is ideally suited to it. This, too, is a good reason for considering Cratylus the more important of Socrates' two interlocutors. But finally, precisely because of these facts about the positions discussed, Plato makes Cratylus a participant throughout the entire dialogue, even when he keeps him silent.

Much that Socrates says to Hermogenes is meant for Cratylus, but Cratylus appears to listen only to those portions with which he agrees. Did Plato want to demonstrate how the prior adherence to a position makes for selective listening and that only through an active exchange of question and answer is it possible to make a dent on the mind of another? What Cratylus hears and remembers is that names, like statements, are either true or false (385c); what he does not observe is that Socrates goes on to shift the discussion to the activity of naming. In this way Socrates begins to "set up" his major opponent in the dialogue. Like a good boxer, he maneuvers him into a position in which his chin is completely exposed to the knockout punch. From that moment on, we must imagine Cratylus on the sidelines, nodding, smiling, and rubbing his hands in delighted agreement, until he finally breaks his silence with, of all things, a quotation from the *Iliad:*

> *Illustrious Ajax, son of Telamon, lord of the people*
> *You appear to have spoken in all things much to my mind.*[31]

And to render the agreement doubly dubious, it is Ajax, none other, to whom Socrates is compared. The punch strikes home. The smile disappears from Cratylus' face, as swiftly, efficiently,

30. "A Criticism of Plato's *Cratylus*," pp. 330–331.
31. 428c4–5; Homer *Iliad* 9. 644f.

and without mercy, Socrates demolishes the nature theory of
names once and for all. Let the reader who nodded with
Cratylus learn his lesson.

The long section in which Socrates invents etymologies—
both plausible ones and others that are plainly ludicrous—
functions, at least in part, to lead Cratylus and fellow travelers
by the nose. That Socrates is not serious for long stretches of
this section is not difficult to see; the tone alone and the utter
implausibility of some of Socrates' etymological concoctions
are good evidence of this. But note these other marks as well.
Hermogenes wants examples of the "natural fitness of
names,"[32] but Socrates "has none to show," having already
said that he "knew nothing" (391a4–6). An inquiry into the
matter is then proposed—but one that a more serious Socrates
would certainly not approve of. Authorities are to be called
upon. And while Protagoras is rejected (by Hermogenes, not
by Socrates!) because that Sophist's doctrine has just been dis-
credited, Hermogenes "must learn from Homer and the poets"
(391c8–d1). A fine source of knowledge for the Plato who
banned Homer from his Republic![33] Somewhat later on,
Hesiod is also brought in and, with his aid, Socrates claims
that wisdom comes to him "all in an instant" (396c7). Instant
wisdom for the proponent of the dialectical method of inquiry? Indeed, it turns out that the long lecture he is giving
was perhaps inspired by the long lecture that the great
Euthyphro had given him, beginning at dawn that morning.[34]
"His wisdom and enchanting ravishment," says Socrates, "have

---

32. τὴν φύσει ὀρθότητα ὀνόματος. Note the nice ambiguity of the
phrase; it is apt both for Socrates' and Cratylus' type of fitness.

33. See also the *Ion,* an early dialogue.

34. On the "utility" of long lectures, see *Protagoras* 334c–e. Socrates'
interpretation of Simonides' poem in that dialogue plays a role similar to
the section on etymologies here. In both, fun is made of the appeal to
authorities and of the confusion that arises if one goes on at too great
length without examining what one is saying. Both passages, too, are
relatively light interludes before the serious arguments of the final sections of the dialogue. See Ch. 2, especially Sec. VII.

not only filled my ears, but taken possession of my soul" (396d7–8).[35] Nor are we allowed to forget that Socrates is under a special influence, for we are reminded of that at several subsequent points.[36] Cratylus is indeed led astray (as is Hermogenes, for that matter), but Plato's readers should not be.

And yet, throughout the section, Socrates has his sober moments. Repeatedly in this etymological mélange, Socrates shows considerable awareness of how a language actually develops. No account of Plato's theory of language can afford to neglect the surprisingly empirical attitude that is at times expressed in this long passage, so rich in things sensible and silly. Socrates thinks of a language as changing as time goes by; he is cognizant of the fact that different dialects use different sounds and letters to say the same thing; he speculates that letters are added or dropped for the sake of euphony.[37] Not only is there a display of an almost un-Greek sense of history here, but in so far as foreign (barbarian) languages are not treated as inferior to Greek, a customary Greek provincialism is overcome as well. But aside from what all this tells us of Plato's thinking about language, these scattered passages play a particular role in the dialogue under discussion. For there Socrates makes clear, with the aid of specific instances, that what makes a sound a name is that we *understand* it as such. Whatever the *ideal* language may be like, *actual* languages are a product of custom. We communicate thought to each other by means of names, because in each language, dialect, or period the sounds and letters that are used belong to an entire community. Neither Hermogenes with his Humpty Dumpty view nor Cratylus with his strict representationalism is correct about the nature of actual, ordinary languages. Moreover,

---

35. Whether or not the Euthyphro who inspired Socrates here is the "theologian" of the dialogue which bears that name, we can be sure that the inspiration of his long lecture fell considerably short of the divine.

36. E.g., 399a, 407d, 410e, 411b, 413d, 420d.

37. E.g., 395e, 398b–c, 398d, 402c–403a, 409d–e, 414c, 418a–419b, 421c–d.

while dialectic would benefit from expert linguistic legislation, it does not absolutely require it, provided a community of philosophers shares a language that can serve as the medium of investigation.

Cratylus does not pay heed to these hints scattered throughout the section on etymologies or he would not have thought that Socrates was an oracle, giving answers very much to his mind (428c). He hears, instead, how Socrates proposes to derive the flux of Heracleitus from such marks as the rolling character of the sound designated by the letter *rho* and the rest of Parmenides from the way in which the tongue is stopped when it pronounces *delta* or *tau*. That Socrates later repudiates these alleged metaphysical implications of the sounds of names should not surprise us, if we recall that he had introduced this last part of the etymological section with this disclaimer: "My first notions of original names are truly wild and ridiculous, though I have no objection to imparting them to you if you desire" (426b5–7). No doubt Cratylus thought that Socrates was being unduly modest. But no doubt, too, Cratylus deserved the unpleasant surprise that jarred him out of his complacency.

In all probability Plato uses the opportunity provided by the etymology section to poke fun at various other theorists of language of his own time and of the recent past. Perhaps the great Prodicus' fifty-drachma course is satirized more than we shall ever know. The main point of this portion of the dialogue must nevertheless be accounted for by the purpose of the *Cratylus* as a whole. It both reveals Socrates' views about the actual state of naming and cites particular examples of the absurdity of Cratylus' doctrine. But given the manner in which the section is written, it will be understood in one way by an adherent of Cratylus' rigid representational nature theory of naming and in quite another by one whose mind is not in this way closed. If one overlooks its somewhat excessive length, Socrates' inspired etymological outburst can thus readily be seen as a method of tying together the different parts of the dialogue. Here Plato *exhibits* what is elsewhere stated; he uses the playwright's subtle device and characterizes the personages he has created not only by what they themselves are given to say but by their reactions to the words of others.

VI. CODA AND CONCLUSION (439a–440e)

The *Cratylus* is a single, unified work devoted to an exploration of the relationship of language to the pursuit of knowledge. While the coda at the dialogue's close goes beyond this theme, it nonetheless confirms this view of the work's unity.

Hermogenes' position is not a position on language at all; if he were right, communication of any sort would be impossible. Language must at least be given in law; a conversation can be carried on only by investigators who share the same linguistic customs. Socrates does not so much refute Hermogenes as replace his essentially skeptical doctrine with a suggestion of his own. Language is a means to knowledge: the function of names in inquiry must be built into the very conception of names.

The danger to knowledge that comes from Cratylus' side is both more serious and more complex. As a *means* to knowledge, Cratylus' names are useless. They reduce a man engaged in inquiry to silence or require him to speak only the whole truth. Against this doctrine Socrates levels his most destructive arguments, for names are needed in the enterprise of dialectic.

But Cratylus goes much further. For him, names are not means at all; they are themselves the very objects of knowledge. A two-pronged response must be made to this, of which the second calls for considerations that go far beyond language.

The first task is negative and requires showing that we cannot confine our inquiry to names and in this way expect to learn about the nature of the things named. The last two arguments against Cratylus (435d–438e), we saw, were devoted to this, and they yield the conclusion that "the knowledge of things is not to be derived from names. No; they must rather be studied and investigated in their connection with one another" (439b6–8). But what is it, then, that we do know and how *is* knowing possible? By converting means into the end—names as instruments into objects of knowledge—questions are raised about that end itself.

Plato closes the dialogue by briefly widening his focus from the narrow topic of names to take a glance at the larger problems that must also be dealt with if knowledge is to be seen as possible. But it is only a glance; he makes sure that we are not deluded into believing that such issues can be settled within the compass of a few pages.

"If everything is in a state of transition and there is nothing abiding" (440a6–7), knowledge cannot be. On the one hand, the objects of knowledge must remain what they are, or even as we say that they are "that or of such a kind," they will "no longer be 'thus,' while the word is in our mouths" (439d9–11). If the power of knowing, on the other hand, "is liable to change, then it will be transformed into something other than knowing, and knowing will thereby cease to exist" (440a9–b2). As in Heracleitus' view of the world, "there will be no one to know and nothing to be known" (440b3–4).

In sharp contrast to this, Socrates often dreams that there is "some permanent nature of goodness, beauty, and several other things" (439c7–d1). And while he admits that it may be true that "all things leak like a pot, or that the whole external world is afflicted with rheum and catarrh" (440c8–d2), he thinks that it may also very likely be untrue.

Socrates urges Cratylus to reflect further on these matters (440d). The latter, however, declares that he has already accepted the doctrine of Heracleitus (440d–e). Just as Cratylus' position on names is incompatible with dialectic as a means to knowledge, so his Heracleitean leanings call into question the possibility of knowledge altogether. But Plato's Socrates is aware of the magnitude and complexity of the problem. "I hope," says Cratylus, bidding farewell to Socrates, "that you will continue to think about these things yourself" (440e6–7), and we know that Plato will devote a long lifetime to doing so.

2

The Way of Socrates and the Way of Protagoras

I. INTRODUCTION

While the *Protagoras* is one of Plato's most dramatic dialogues, nothing could be more misleading than to look upon it as a philosophic conversation dressed up in literary costume. Philosophy and drama, here, are one; like a playwright, Plato makes no statements of his own. Indeed, when, at the end of the work, he has Socrates declare that the subject is in "utter confusion" (361c3),[1] he reminds us that we are not to take away from the dialogue some principle its author takes to have been established. Instead, Plato depicts and exhibits his theme in the *Protagoras:* he pits against each other the ways of Socrates and Protagoras and lets us see how Socrates teaches Protagoras a lesson—that of the necessity of philosophy.

The main conversation is between Socrates and Protagoras; but several additional characters make important contributions to the dialogue, while still others are made to play their particular roles in silence. By individuating the speech of his characters and by describing them, by providing stage directions and by ordering his cast into scenes, Plato gives individ-

---

1. For the most part, I shall cite the *Protagoras* translation by W. K. C. Guthrie, *Protagoras and Meno* (Harmondsworth: Penguin Classics, 1956). Copyright by W. K. C. Guthrie, 1956. The translation is cited by permission of Penguin Books Ltd.

ual life to Socrates and Protagoras and, in varying degrees, to their companions. The chief business of the work, of course, is talk; but the range of that is also great. There are serious arguments and eloquent speeches; there is polite chitchat and wrangling; there are bursts of anger and exchanges of compliments; and there is humor.

While a staging of the *Protagoras* would be an entertaining spectacle, it is far more than that. The long speeches and dialectical arguments, the manner of speaking and gestures, the physical movement and setting are all dramatic elements contributing to the philosophic purpose of the whole. In the *Protagoras,* Plato depicts two styles of life, the Philosopher's and the Sophist's. At the center of his concern is the nature of the good life as each of the chief protagonists regards it: their respective conceptions of morality. But since both Socrates and Protagoras are serious about their roles as teachers, Plato's picture also contains what each of them takes to be the correct mode of inquiry into the important questions of morality and what it means for them to teach the young men of Greece who come to them to learn how to be men of excellence. Moreover, for Plato, philosophy is lived as much as thought and spoken. The depiction of the ways of Socrates and Protagoras includes a portrait of the two masters, of their attitudes to their own work, their students, the variegated audience assembled, and toward each other. In the dialogue, Plato paints a double portrait of the most important educators of fifth-century Greece.[2]

---

2. The dialogue takes place toward the end of Protagoras' career and near the beginning of Socrates'. It is a time of peace in Greece. This (as well as other evidence) puts its dramatic date just a few years before Plato's birth—say, 433 or 432 B.C. See A. E. Taylor, *Plato: The Man and His Work* (New York: Meridian reprint of the 6th ed., 1956), p. 236. See also Hermann Sauppe, *Protagoras* ("Platons Ausgewählte Dialoge," Vol. II [Berlin: Weidmannsche Buchhandlung, 1884]), pp. 10–12 and others.

There is wide agreement that Plato wrote the dialogue early in his career—surely some time before the *Republic,* but there is little to suggest just precisely where in the first group of Socratic dialogues the *Protagoras* belongs. For an overview on the ordering of the dialogues, see David Ross, *Plato's Theory of Ideas* (Oxford: Clarendon Press, 1951), pp. 1–10.

Yet analogies drawn from portraiture must remain incomplete, for there is movement in the *Protagoras* with which painting cannot cope: there is Socrates' lesson. In spite of the fact that no thesis is established in the dialogue, there is a decisive outcome of the struggle in which Socrates and Protagoras are engaged.

Protagoras' way is to use the powers of reason and reflection to make explicit the beliefs and aspirations of men as they are and to teach virtue by formulating what is already embedded in the practices of the societies from which his students come. For Socrates, the knowledge of how to live one's life calls for a more fundamental inquiry into the nature of man and his good. But as Protagoras' unambitious common sense view of man and morality is examined, it is progressively revealed that beneath *it,* too, lurks a philosophic position. The Sophist who eschews philosophy *has* a philosopy and must learn to deal with it philosophically. In the presence of his fellow-Sophists and their followers and of young Hippocrates, a would-be pupil, Protagoras is taught by Socrates that philosophy is necessary. This chapter will attempt to show how the many components of the *Protagoras* function to achieve the complex purpose of the dialogue.

II. The Opening (309a–320c)

1. After the Encounter with Protagoras (309a–310a)

At the work's opening, Socrates meets an unnamed friend to whom he appears as if he had just come from the "pursuit of the captivating Alcibiades" (309a2). That handsome youth was indeed part of the company Socrates has just left. But so was Protagoras, and in the discussion that Socrates had with that "wisest man now living" (309d2), Alcibiades was often forgotten altogether. "Must not perfect wisdom take the palm for handsomeness?" (309c11–12).

In this initial characterization of Protagoras, there is both irony and truth. The Sophist does not have "perfect wisdom," but discussion with him is a far greater attraction than erotic banter even with Alcibiades. Thus we learn not only of Socrates' predilections but also of Protagoras' ability to engage his audience. From the beginning, we are invited to assume a complex attitude toward the great Sophist. Protagoras, by no means all that wise, is nonetheless depicted as an able thinker and a man of considerable nobility. He secures the adherence and admiration of the elite of Athens and serves as an eloquent spokesman for its views. It will become clear that Protagoras is an opponent of consequence, a most philosophical defender of unphilosophy.

At the very end of the dialogue, Socrates goes off to keep a previous appointment, by then much delayed by his conversation with Protagoras. If the encounter with the friend which we hear about at the opening of the work is that engagement, the original purpose of that meeting is now put aside so that Socrates can give an account of his discussion with Protagoras. In this way Plato allows Socrates not only to report what was said in the course of the morning, but also to describe the participants' appearance, actions, and tone of voice. Nevertheless, Socrates also remains a character: his part, too, is written out, no less than that of Protagoras. Socrates' own arguments and speeches and his description of others are all the invention of the author of the dialogue; it is Plato's Socrates who reveals himself in everything he says.

The unnamed friend is anxious to hear about the conversation with Protagoras, while Socrates is grateful to have an opportunity to tell his tale.

2. Hippocrates (310a–313c)

Before daybreak and with much noise, Hippocrates had roused Socrates. Protagoras has just arrived in Athens, and Hippocrates now needs help in persuading the great Sophist to take him on as a pupil, in spite of his youth. Only in this scene at dawn do we hear Hippocrates speak, for throughout the long debate between Socrates and Protagoras he remains silent.

Still, Hippocrates is a worthy prize of the battle that is waged between the two educators. Later he is introduced to Protagoras as coming from a "great and prosperous family" and as being "considered the equal of any of his contemporaries in natural gifts" (316b9–10), and we know by then that these claims are just. Hippocrates has money enough to pay Protagoras' high fee or at the least he has friends who will come to his assistance (311d). He is open and natural: he does not disguise his eagerness and is quick to blush (312a). We see him display wit: when Socrates asks whether Protagoras has harmed him, only a practiced tongue could summon the quick response that Protagoras has done so by failing to share his wisdom with Hippocrates (310d). And in discussion with Socrates, he shows himself to be intelligent. Hippocrates and Socrates, furthermore, are well acquainted. Socrates recognizes the voice that wakes him up (310b), while Hippocrates mentions that he had meant to tell Socrates that he had to leave Athens briefly to go after a runaway slave (310c). And yet, there is no evidence at all that Hippocrates has hitherto learned anything from associating with Socrates. His education appears to have been confined to the tutoring of gymnasts and music masters; the Athenian oligarchy could not offer more to its sons. Hippocrates is thus unschooled and untrained, but well-intentioned, talented, and wealthy—the very best of Athenian youth and an ideal novice for a teacher.

Since it is too early to go to the house of Callias where Protagoras is staying, Socrates introduces the main theme of the dialogue and asks Hippocrates what he expects to learn were he to become the Sophist's pupil. Physicians, sculptors, or poets, when they teach, impart their own crafts to their pupils, so that these may, in turn, become physicians, sculptors, or poets. Hippocrates' blush comes when the implication of this becomes explicit, for he does not wish to become a professional Sophist. The shame is taken for granted; the respect and

admiration Protagoras evokes does not go so far as to make his
métier quite respectable for a gentleman, or so at least Plato
means to convey. Hippocrates is much happier with the suggestion that he merely wants to continue the sort of liberal
education he received from the masters who taught him in
school.

But the problem is not solved by this retreat from professional status as a goal of education; we still do not know what
the Sophist teaches. Nor is it enough to think of him as the
"master of the art of making clever speakers" (312d6–7), for
the subject matter of those speakers' discourses must be the
same as that of which the Sophist, their teacher, has knowledge. And this is just what we do not know. Hippocrates' eagerness to be Protagoras' pupil is thus not matched by an
awareness of what will become of him if his wish is granted.
Socrates, therefore, impresses upon him the gravity of the step
he aims to take. In buying food for the body, no great risk is
incurred; one can still seek advice as to whether and how one
ought to consume it. "But knowledge cannot be taken away
in a parcel. When you have paid for it you must receive it
straight into the soul" (314b1–3). Afterwards, it is too late to
inquire into the good or harm the teaching might have done.

Socrates' urgent concern reveals that he understands the
nature of Protagoras' teaching. When Hippocrates of Cos or
Phidias of Athens teach the crafts of healing or sculpting, their
pupils retain the option *not* to use the skills they have acquired or to use them in one way rather than another. Protagoras, however, does not merely add to his pupils' repertoire
of skills; he changes them in a more fundamental way by transforming them permanently as *persons*. The problem is a serious one: Protagoras and his company of older and wiser men
will have to be consulted.

In the short paragraph that it takes Plato to get the two
young men into the presence of Protagoras at Callias' house,
he manages to reveal a good deal about them and about Sophists. However eager Hippocrates is to meet Protagoras and
however urgent Socrates considers the problem they plan to

discuss with the Sophist to be, the two men continue a discussion they had begun *en route,* even after they reach their destination. "We were standing in the doorway until we should reach agreement" (314c6–7). The contrast with Protagoras is sharp, for at the end of the dialogue to come, he is prepared, in spite of the confusion on the subject closest to his own professional activity, "to turn to other things" (361e6). The attainment of truth, for Protagoras—at least in so far as it is measured by the agreement of two minds joined in inquiry—is never quite the primary aim of the discussion.

Before they get inside, Hippocrates' earlier blush receives some justification. The reputation of Sophists among those who are not self-styled "intellectual leaders of Greece" (337d4), to use Hippias' phrase, is not especially good. With a "Ha, Sophists!" the porter slams the door in their faces "with both hands!" (314d3–4). It takes another try and their assurance that they are not Sophists before Socrates and Hippocrates are brought into the presence.

3. The Cast (314e–316b)

Everyone is there and decorously arranged in groups. The first is dominated by the elderly Protagoras playing *premier danseur.* Six men attend him, all ranged in a long line. On one side are Callias, host and friend of Protagoras, one of the richest men in Athens, who some years later will play a role as diplomat; Paralus, the younger son of Pericles; and Plato's uncle, Charmides, aristocrat and friend of Socrates.[3] Flanking the Sophist on the other side are Xanthippus, the elder of Pericles' sons; Philippides, son of Philomelus who seems to have enjoyed the company of philosophers and Sophists and later sent his son to the school of Plato's rival as teacher, Isocrates; and Antimoerus of Mende, only known through this dialogue and

---

3. The personages of the *Protagoras* can be identified with the aid of standard reference works, although the extent and reliability of our knowledge about them vary greatly.

there identified as a promising pupil of Protagoras who plans to become a Sophist himself. A group of unnamed Athenians and foreigners follow behind, listening to the conversation. All perform their steps with skill, for no one gets in front of Protagoras: "when he and those with him turn round, the listeners divided this way and that in perfect order, and executing a circular movement took their places each time in the rear. It was beautiful" (315b5–8). Music is not entirely absent from this ballet. Protagoras' voice is likened to that of Orpheus, for the foreigners from every city of Greece follow him spellbound, charmed by his voice (315a–b). Music and dance: Protagoras is depicted as an entertainer long before he is so characterized openly, and the contrast with the way of philosophy is drawn explicitly.

The difference between the scene confronting Socrates and the real world of philosophy is then implied more nastily. " 'After that I recognized' . . . Hippias of Elis" (315b9–c1), Socrates quotes from the *Odyssey*. Odysseus has descended to the underworld and perhaps that cantankerous porter was Cerberus. Hippias, ready to speak on any subject and skilled in many crafts, who, when older, will become rich and famous as a teacher, is holding forth on natural science. Asking questions of the polymath are Eryximachus, the physician who, in the *Symposium*, cures Aristophanes of hiccups; Phaedrus, a member of Socrates' circle, represented in the *Phaedrus* as nonetheless a passionate lover of rhetoric; Andron, son of Androtion, a student of Sophists who will have a political careeer; and various foreigners.

" 'And there too spied I Tantalus' " (315c8). Prodicus of Ceos, the man who became wealthy by teaching about words, is subjected to a Homeric torture. Sitting up in bed, Prodicus converses with numerous devotees; and even though Socrates is eager to hear him,[4] he does not, alas, succeed, for Prodicus has so booming a voice that it drowns out the very words he

---

4. In the *Cratylus*, Socrates reports that he could only afford Prodicus' one-drachma course (*Cratylus* 384b). See Ch. 2, p. 17, above.

speaks. Whether those who are listening to the man of fine verbal distinctions can understand him, Socrates does not say, though he tells us who they are: young Agathon, who in time will become a great tragedian and who also figures in the *Symposium;* Pausanias from Cerameis, who admires the poet, but probably for his good looks above all; Adeimantus, son of Cepis, who gains immortality solely from having been made a part of this fictional assemblage; and Adeimantus, son of Leucolophides, who will later have both a military and a political career associated with Alcibiades. There are a few others who are not named.

Two more visitors arrive shortly after Socrates and Hippocrates: Critias, also an aristocratic member of Socrates' circle, an orator and poet, destined to play a leading role among the Thirty Tyrants who later ruled Athens for a year; and Alcibiades, now a young man close to Socrates, later a figure whose brilliant and erratic political and military career will dominate Athenian affairs for more than a decade. Thus assembled in Callias' house is a good sampling of the best young men who live in Athens, both native-born and foreign. The three Sophists, Protagoras, Hippias, and Prodicus, of whom the first is the oldest and most famous, serve as foci. Their mission is to provide a higher education for such men—outstanding in wealth, family, and talent—as surround them.

Although it is still early in the morning, Callias' house is buzzing with conversation. Protagoras and his colleagues must be seen as responding to a strongly felt need for education. In this brief scene Plato shows that when the voice of Socrates enters to compete with that of the Sophists, the debate cannot be regarded merely as entertainment for connoisseurs of speeches and arguments. The ways of Protagoras and Socrates clash not only over the soul of Hippocrates, but over the mind of Greece.

4. The Question (316b–320c)

Socrates is fully at ease in this great company. He introduces Hippocrates, telling Protagoras that they wish to discuss the young man's enrollment as his pupil. Protagoras should decide whether the conversation is to be public or private.

In a dignified speech—as befits an eminently successful practitioner (older by far than anyone else present)—Protagoras opts for a conversation in the open. His own position, after all, differs from that of his forbears. In ancient times, Sophists "adopted a disguise and worked under cover" (316d6): the poets—Homer, Hesiod, and Simonides; religious teachers—Orpheus and Musaeus; physical trainers—Iccus of Tarentum and Herodicus of Selymbra; musicians—Agathocles and Pytholides of Ceos. All of them were really Sophists (we are surprised by the list), hiding under their better-known professions from the malice and resentment of men. Protagoras' claim seems grandiose. Who, if he had fame at all, was *not* a Sophist? Socrates and Hippocrates had led us to think of the Sophists as practitioners of a specialized craft that was to be *contrasted* with poetry, priestcraft, gymnastics, music, and so on; of a *techné* that has its own nature and is governed by principles belonging to it alone. But when he traces his lineage as he does, Protagoras identifies himself, instead, as one of the many sorts of men who have always educated Greece. We are thus subtly warned not to expect a radical departure from tradition in his conception of education.

While prudence might dictate to Protagoras that he should avoid the hostility of men of power by also disguising his profession, he reports that he has not come to harm by working in the open, but has, in fact, prospered. Moreover, he mysteriously hints that he has "devised other precautions" (317b6–7) —other than the frank avowal of his role as Sophist. Surely this safeguard can only be the essential conservatism of a teaching that remains fully at the service of the established order. No Sophist was put to death by a Greek city. Rather, it is the rationalism of Socrates' way which will be regarded as subversive. Socrates will ultimately face the danger of which Protagoras speaks. Bravely, then, where there is no need for bravery, Protagoras prefers to have his "say in front of the

whole company" (317c4–5), though Socrates suspects that he
wants to display his skill to all those assembled, particularly
to his rival Sophists. Callias, host and man of executive ability,
arranges the entire company in a circle and the discussion
begins.

What effect, Socrates wishes to know, will Protagoras' teaching have on young Hippocrates? He would be better each day
than he was the day before. This answer, immediately given,
is of course unsatisfactory, unless we are told in what respect,
at doing what. Pupils of painters become better at painting;
of flute players, at playing the flute.

Protagoras teaches "the proper care of [a man's] personal
affairs, so that he may best manage his own household, and
also of the state's affairs, so as to become a real power in the
city, both as speaker and man of action" (318e5–319a2). This
is precisely what men come to learn from him and, presumably, why they also study with Hippias. His rival, however,
does not give them what they want, but imposes on them such
specialized subjects as "arithmetic and astronomy and geometry and music" (318e2–3). Protagoras seeks to contrast the
unity of his subject as he conceives it with the diversity of
Hippias' curriculum.[5] Another theme is thus introduced, for
Hippias' unintegrated polymathy is also subjected to a critique
in the course of the dialogue,[6] although the main contest remains that between Socrates and Protagoras.

Socrates, for the present, does not inquire further into the
subject matter that Protagoras professes, but accepts it as the
art of politics. He merely wonders about its teachability and,
using Protagoras' own technique, supports his skepticism with
three reasons that rest upon Athenian beliefs and practices.
Neither the nature of the subject matter to be taught nor a
conception of what it is to teach are brought into the picture.

---

5. And in doing so, he amusingly singles out the fields that will play
so important a part in the education of the philosopher in the *Republic*.
6. See p. 120.

First, Athenians do not acknowledge the existence of experts in politics. Their assemblies will only listen to trained specialists when decisions are to be made about architectural projects or ship building. Yet everyone is free to debate governmental policy, whether he be rich or poor, shoemaker or ship owner. Since in political matters, no one objects to anyone's lack of expertise, Athenians cannot think that politics can be taught.

Second, those who are wise in politics make no attempt to teach their sons the "art" they have acquired. Even Pericles' own sons here were not subjected to an education in politics, but "simply browse around on their own like sacred cattle, on the chance of picking up virtue automatically" (320a2–3). Thus, as individuals, even the wisest Athenians cannot believe that political virtue can be taught.

Finally, when now and then someone thinks it possible to teach the art of politics after all, the attempt to provide a special education proves unsuccessful. Good men have not, as a matter of fact, succeeded in making anyone else better.

Socrates' faith in this negative conclusion is to some degree shaken by a single *ad hominem* argument: so great a man as Protagoras believes otherwise. He *must* impart his wisdom.

Socrates is not ironic. What Protagoras thinks is virtue cannot, in Socrates' opinion, be taught—at least not according to Socrates' conception of what it is to teach. Nor are Socrates' reservations based on his *own* understanding of virtue as "the proper care of . . . [a man's] personal affairs" (318e4–5), since for Socrates, *vox populi,* even when it is Athenian, is not the measure of what virtue is. Neither Pericles and other leaders of the Athenian democracy nor the best young men assembled in Callias' house can serve as models of excellence for Socrates.[7] What is *believed* to be virtue may rightly be thought not to be teachable, but the nature of virtue itself remains unexamined.

---

7. For a scathing assessment of Pericles, see what Plato's Socrates has to say about him in *Gorgias* 515e–516d.

On one level, then, there is genuine disagreement between the two protagonists. Protagoras takes virtue—as it is popularly thought of—to be teachable, while Socrates does not. At the same time, we must remain aware that Socrates' (call it philosophic) conception of virtue has not even been introduced into the dialogue. Thus, no debate about its teachability is as yet possible.

III. THE GREAT SPEECH (320c–328d)

So far, the only evidence we have of Protagoras' greatness is what we know of his reputation; but now we shall hear from Protagoras himself. The magnificence of his speech makes it clear that Plato did not mean to set up a straw man for his Socrates to knock down. The best representation of the old way is pitted against the way of Socrates. Nevertheless, it does not follow that Plato's Protagoras is faithful to the historical original or that we are given a sympathetic exposition *ab intra* of the Protagorean position. Regardless of what its originator might have thought important, Plato—philosopher, not historian—portrays the side of Protagoreanism that was central for him. It pays to remind oneself that the *Protagoras* is a dramatic work: all those who speak in it are fictional characters even when they bear the names of historical personages. They say nothing of their own (they *are* nothing on their own), but only what suits the purpose of the creator and sole author of their words.[8] Thus it is *Plato's* Protagoras who now speaks.

The audience encourages Protagoras to expound his views in the manner he prefers. Considering a story to be more pleasant, he begins, "Once upon a time . . ." (320c8), and tells the

---

8. For a discussion of the problem of finding the historical Protagoras behind such treatments as Plato's, see Eric A. Havelock, *The Liberal Temper in Greek Politics* (New Haven: Yale University Press, 1957), pp. 156ff. The *Protagoras* is extensively discussed in Chs. IV, VII, and VIII.

tale of the creation of all the mortal species. The gods had assigned to Epimetheus and Prometheus the task of equipping all creatures for life on earth. The two agreed that the former would distribute the various capacities and that the latter would review his work. Not being overly bright, Epimetheus, in dispensing the different characteristics and powers that would enable the animal world to survive, exhausted all such capacities before he reached the human race. Prometheus' assistance was called for, and even he had to resort to theft. From Hephaestus he stole fire and the art of working with it, and from Athena he stole the other arts. He then distributed them, one art to some men, another to others. But political wisdom "was in the keeping of Zeus" (321d5), beyond Prometheus' reach.

Thus endowed, men were able to shelter themselves and to extract food from the earth. Soon they were also led to invent speech and, because they shared in the divine, they became the only creatures to engage in religious practices.[9] Yet men could not survive without political skill. Individually, they were too weak to stand up against the natural strength of beasts. But war, even war on animals, was not available to them, for it is a part of the political art. An attempt to find safety in fortified cities foundered on strife.

Fearing that the human race would soon become extinct, Zeus sent Hermes "to impart to men the qualities of respect for others (*aidôs*) and a sense of justice (*dikê*)" (322c1–2).[10] And because cities could not survive if, as in the case of specialized skills, only a few possessed these political traits, all

---

9. If one reads διὰ τὴν τοῦ θεοῦ συγγένειαν (322a4) as referring to the divine arts shared by men, there is no inconsistency, as Havelock supposes (*ibid.*, p. 92), in the fact that other (nonreligious) beings are also creatures of God. See Gregory Vlastos, ed., *Plato's Protagoras* (Library of Liberal Arts 59 [Indianapolis: Bobbs-Merrill, 1956]), p. ix, n. 11 (henceforth cited as *Vlastos, 1956*).

10. On this interpretative translation of Guthrie's, see n. 14, below.

men were to be given their share. Thus we see why Athenians and all other men believe that only a few can advise on architectural matters and such, whereas in political affairs "they listen to every man's opinion" (323a2).

In the second part of his speech, Protagoras claims that virtue, that is, the art of politics, is taught—moreover, not only by him, but by everyone. An understanding of it thus calls for some clarification of the conception of human nature which functions in Protagoras' anthropological myth.

Before men are brought forth from the earth, all the types of characteristics that animals need to survive have already been used up: physical features such as fur, claws, sharp teeth; powers such as the ability to run, fly, and swim; instinctual capacities such as the propensity to build nests or dig burrows. All these Epimethean traits belong to animals by nature; they are not taught. On men, Prometheus then bestows the gift of the arts, so that they can provide themselves with clothes, shoes, beds, and arms.[11] But, clearly, this contribution was not made in the manner in which Epimetheus had given out wings and fins; men, even those destined to be shoemakers, are not literally *born* knowing how to make shoes. And yet, Prometheus' gift includes more than the *disposition to acquire* the various arts. Protagoras in no way qualifies his report that Prometheus gave to men "wisdom in the arts" (321d1). Moreover, had Prometheus done any less than that, the problem created by Epimetheus' obtuseness would not have been solved, for men can no more survive on earth with just the disposition to acquire the arts than they can without it. Thus in addition to this disposition, Prometheus' gift needed to include an arrangement for its *actualization*. He gave to men the capacity to acquire such arts as making clothes and shoes *and* he made sure that the lives of men would be so arranged that

---

11. Before Prometheus entered the picture, men were described as "naked, unshod, unbedded, and unarmed" (321c5–6).

they would in fact become craftsmen and pass on their skills from generation to generation by means of teaching.[12]

In one important respect, Hermes' gift of *aidôs* and *dikê* differs from Prometheus' donation of the arts, for Hermes makes his contribution to *all* men. Zeus orders universal distribution, because only then will respect for others and justice "bring order into our cities and create a bond of friendship" (322c3). Those incapable of acquiring a share are to be put to death. Moreover, men expect everyone at least to *profess* to be good, holding that "whoever does not make such a claim is out of his mind, for a man cannot be without some share in justice, or he would not be human" (323b6–c2). Men may be magnificently virtuous or abysmally evil, but unless they understand that they ought to prefer good to evil, they are not men at all. Civic virtue, then, is a part of human nature; any creature lacking it belongs to the world of prehuman amoral savages.

In other respects, however, Hermes' gift is perfectly analogous to that of Prometheus. *Aidôs* and *dikê* themselves are said to be given to men, not merely the potentiality to acquire them. "Zeus . . . sent Hermes to impart to men *aidô te kai dikên*" (322c2).[13] But Hermes does not dispense civic virtue in the way Epimetheus dispenses fur and wings. Men are not born knowing and observing the customs of their cities: Hermes' contribution of respect for others and justice thus also consists of two components. On the one hand, the god must give to each man the capacity to acquire the knowledge of how to act vis à vis other men and, on the other, he must make sure that men considered collectively will actually develop specific modes of moral behavior and pass on their customs and practices from one generation to the next. The first of

---

12. Propagation of the arts requires the universal possession of language, even though the specialized crafts are only selectively distributed among men. The universality of language thus does not constitute an inconsistency in Protagoras' myth. See Havelock, *The Liberal Temper*, p. 93.

13. Also see the passages to follow.

these is akin to the moral sense of which some have spoken when describing Hermes' gift and might be called the psychological component of civic virtue, while the second might be referred to as the sociological aspect of civic virtue. Neither by itself suffices: there must be the ability to learn and there must be teaching.[14] Appropriately, then, the latter part of Protagoras' speech treats of the teaching of virtue.

To begin with, all men *believe* that virtue is taught and not conferred by nature. No one is blamed or punished for being "ugly or dwarfish or weak. . . . Everyone knows that it is nature or chance which gives this kind of characteristics to a man . . ." (323d3–5). By contrast, vice—"everything that is contrary to civic virtue" (324a1)—gives rise to admonition, precisely because it is believed that "virtue can be acquired" (324a2–3). And a closer look at the nature of punishment yields further confirmation. Rational men punish "for the sake of the future, to prevent either the same man or, by the spectacle of his punishment, someone else, from doing wrong again" (324b4–5). Implicit in this view of punishment is the belief "that virtue can be instilled by education" (324b5–6).

But if virtue is taught, who teaches it? All men must have a share of virtue if there is to be a state at all; this quality "must enter into every man's action whatever other occupation

---

14. G. B. Kerford, in "Protagoras' Doctrine of Justice and Virtue in the *Protagoras* of Plato," *The Journal of Hellenic Studies*, 73 (1953), 42–45, rightly maintains that Hermes confers *aidôs* and *dikê* themselves and correctly objects to those who think that he merely gives men the disposition to acquire these virtues. (See, for example, J. A. Stewart, *The Myths of Plato* [London: MacMillan, 1905]: "All men have implanted in them what may be called 'an original moral sense,' which education appeals to and awakens. All men are capable of morality as they are capable of speech" [p. 226].) But while Kerford insists that the method by which men acquire the political art is precisely through the teaching of which Protagoras speaks next, he ignores the fact that a condition for such teaching is the capacity to learn. (One cannot teach parrots to swim.) And this Hermes must also confer. Guthrie's translation of 323c1–2 as "respect for others and a *sense* of justice" is thus misleading, for it is only a *part* of what Hermes gives to men.

he chooses to learn and practice" (325a3–4). If men fail to be virtuous, they must be punished or, should that be unsuccessful, expelled or put to death. Surely, then, all, and especially good, men (who, we have already seen, *believe* that virtue can be taught) teach their sons virtue and, moreover, from earliest childhood. Everyone who comes in contact with children points out to them what is right and wrong, honorable and disgraceful, what is acceptable to the gods and what must not be done. This process continues in school. Moral lessons are contained in the stories and poems children learn. Music masters "instill self-control and deter the young from evil doing" (326a4–5). Even the trainer assists by insuring that weakness will not lead to cowardice. All the virtues shortly to be discussed are thus seen to be taught by the community: justice, holiness, temperance, and courage. Nor is education in virtue limited to the rich, for the very laws of the state act as teachers by requiring all citizens to do what is right, on pain of being punished and corrected.

Finally, Protagoras turns to explain why "many sons of good men turn out worthless" (326e6–7). If flute playing were as essential to society as is virtue and "everyone taught everyone else that art" (327a5), it would not be the sons of the best flute players who would become the most accomplished at that craft, but those with the most talent. In such a flute-playing society, furthermore, the worst player would compare very favorably with someone who knew nothing of the art. And so it is with virtue. The most talented acquire the most of it under our conditions of incessant teaching, while even the worthless sons of great men compare favorably in virtue with uncivilized savages.

Because everyone teaches virtue, Socrates erroneously thinks that no one does. But we learn virtue as we learn Greek, at the hands of many masters. For himself, Protagoras merely claims that he is "only a little better than the others at advancing us on the road to virtue" (328b1–3).

When the speech is over, Socrates sits spellbound at Protagoras' "long and magnificent display of eloquence" (328d3–4).

The praise is deserved, but so is the tinge of irony which is later to be followed up by Socrates' repeated complaints about Protagoras' propensity for making long speeches. With a sure hand and in a felicitous manner, Protagoras has sketched out an anthropological position on the nature and origins of morality. Yet the speech so expertly fashions Protagoras' diverse claims and assumptions into a seamless object that it does not easily serve as the starting point of a philosophic inquiry. The confusion at the end of the dialogue is in good part attributable to this speech, which treats of so many questions all at once.

Reasons that justify the perplexity of two fictional characters depicted as engaged in a continuous discussion nevertheless do not justify confusion in the mind of the dialogue's reader who has the leisure to examine more closely what was said. It will therefore be necessary to comment further on Protagoras' speech before continuing with the exchange between Socrates and Protagoras.

Above all, we must be clear about the nature of Protagoras' civic virtue. *Aidôs* and *dikê* are not described, but we do learn about them by attending to their function. Before Hermes' intervention, men preyed indiscriminately on each other and were incapable of acting in concert; after their distribution men learned to leave each other be and to cooperate in joint ventures. Nothing, however, is said explicitly about how men are enabled to act by means of this new capacity, nor does Protagoras speak of a standard by which it can be judged to function well or poorly. It is assumed, instead, that men simply *can* act in the way they actually *do* and that we find out what is "correct" exercise of civic virtue by analyzing the practices and institutions in and by which men actually succeed in acting together.

No general answer, therefore, is possible to the question of what virtue is. In Athens, to be virtuous is to have the ability to follow Athenian customs and to play one's part in Athenian institutions. To be more or less virtuous means to be a better or worse Athenian, as this is measured by the standards and

goals that are embedded in the practices of that city and its
citizens. Change the focus to Sparta or Crete and the customs
and institutions of those cities become the standards of virtue.
Hermes' civic virtue is not a power that enables men to live a
certain kind of life which may then be actualized more or less
well in different times and places. Rather, the *capacity* to create and perpetuate customs and institutions is intelligible only
within the context of *actual* arrangements. In contemporary
jargon, Protagoras is a naturalist and a relativist.

If virtue in Athens is to do as the Athenians do, then surely
the Athenians are the chief teachers of that virtue. Parents,
nurses, teachers, and the laws of the city teach by example, by
admonition and praise, by prescribing accepted and desired
behavior and by proscribing types of actions that are not
wanted in Athens. And the poets also teach virtue and have
special importance as educators. Not only do their stories de-
pict good men and bad, right acts and wrong (as the Athenians evaluate such things), and thus provide examples of
virtue and vice that are larger than life, but they instill the
sort of attitudes and beliefs that are supportive of good Athenian behavior.

Before beginning his speech, Protagoras had rather star-
tlingly attributed a very distinguished ancestry to his profession
as Sophist. When now he concludes his discourse by saying,
"my claim is that I am one of these, rather better than anyone
else" (328b1–2), the mystery about the group he had originally named is dispelled. Those ancients were—and in their
legacy still are—among the great teachers of Greece in just
the sense Protagoras' speech sketches out. If any mystery remains, it is how Protagoras himself functions as such a teacher
and why he should be better than anyone else.

Part of the answer is that Protagoras teaches virtue in just
the way everyone else does. A child is in apprenticeship to his
Athenian family and teachers just as he might be to the sculptor Phidias or the physician Hippocrates. By watching and
listening, imitating and practicing, by being encouraged and

reproved, he may become a good Athenian, a good sculptor, or a good physician. In effect, such teaching is successful to the extent that it induces the attitudes, inculcates the habits, and imparts the skills that are required for carving marble or reducing fever or conducting the many activities that are called for in the management of one's life and that of the city. At the center of the teacher's function, then, is the job of conditioning. Protagoras could not have the success he claims for himself without doing precisely that. He helps to bring to fruition man's capacity for virtue; this is the psychological side of his role.

Like the teachers in the tradition he acknowledges, Protagoras is engaged in indoctrination. How then does he differ from them, and on what does he base his claim that he is "rather better than anyone else" (328b2)? If one had to answer in a single word, one would say by virtue of "self-consciousness." Unlike parents and nurses, but also unlike the great poets of the past, Protagoras has made it his business to *reflect* upon the practices of men and to make himself aware of what has hitherto remained implicit. Protagoras' great speech itself provides evidence for this. The Athenian people, for example, do this and that; but it is Protagoras who points out that their activities are predicated on the implicit *belief* that virtue can be taught. He seeks to find the principles that are embedded in the practices of a society and to articulate the beliefs men really have (as indicated by what they do), regardless of the opinions they profess. His role is thus different from that of the poets, who do not so much reflect upon the morality of their society as express and epitomize it. And yet, as we shall see in the discussions to come, Protagoras falls short, from Socrates' point of view, of being a philosopher. He does not subject the position of the many to a critique made from the perspective of an independently worked out doctrine. He confines himself, rather, to acting as a reporter of the key propositions that underlie the customs of men. Protagoras the teacher is also a sociologist.

That a stranger to Athens or Sparta should be a superior teacher of Athenian or Lacedaemonian conventions is then not at all surprising[15]—any more than that the Frenchman de Tocqueville should have had excellent insight into the ways of the United States. The sociological bent is made up of good sense, experience, a sharp eye, and the perspective that is gained from not being involved. It is the ability to see general principles amidst a welter of details; to be a stranger may indeed be an advantage. In sum, we have no reason to doubt that Protagoras' fame as teacher was justified.

But so is Socrates' worry in behalf of Hippocrates. Protagoras educates by indoctrinating. And while his method calls for the formulation of general principles, these are neither exhibited as such to the student nor are they supported by argument. Instead, the sociological generalizations that are a product of his observations serve Protagoras as means in a process in which persuasion is essentially manipulatory. Protagoras' pupils are transformed by him without their ever becoming clear how their souls are affected in this encounter with their teacher.

The Sophist's great speech ends with a revealing declaration. "I have adopted the following method of assessing my payment. Anyone who comes to learn from me may either pay the fee I ask for or, if he prefers, go to a temple, state on oath what he believes to be the worth of my instruction, and deposit that amount" (328b5–c2). The odds in this bet are heavily weighted in Protagoras' favor. He counts on his ability to modify the souls of his students and thus on forestalling any loss of the sizable fee he normally collects. Protagoras' confidence here and Socrates' concern for Hippocrates have their root in the very same understanding of what is it for Protagoras to teach. But just as the virtue which Protagoras main-

---

15. A. E. Taylor (*Plato: The Man and His Work*, pp. 246–247) thought it a "paradox" that the stranger from Abdera should teach the virtue of the different communities he visited.

tains is teachable is not virtue in Socrates' view, so what Protagoras understands by teaching is not what teaching means for Socrates.

IV. JUSTICE AND HOLINESS (328d–331e)

Socrates does not remain speechless for long. He has one "small" (328e4) question which Protagoras can surely answer with ease. Unlike popular orators, Protagoras is not only capable of making a "Marathon of a speech" (329b2), but can answer questions and do so briefly. Virtue, in Protagoras' speech, appeared to be a single thing. It would now be good to know whether "justice, temperance, holiness, and the rest" (329c4–5) constitute virtue as parts make up a whole or whether they are different names for the same thing.

This question is not imposed on an innocent Protagoras, nor is it frivolous. The great speech emphatically insisted on the singleness of virtue: "Is there not some *one* thing," Protagoras asks, "in which all citizens must share, if a state is to exist at all?" (324d7–e1). A moment later he refers to "this *one* thing" (324e3) and to "a *single* whole, manly virtue" (325a2).[16] Moreover, the pointed rejection of Hippias' polymathy 318d7–e5) underlines the fact that Protagoras professes to teach a single subject: virtue, for him, is one. And if it *is* one, a disquisition on the nature of its unity would be revealing. Ideally, it would tell us precisely in what way the several virtues *are* virtues, that is, just what characteristic makes them virtues. In turn, such information would shed much light on the teachability of virtue, the subject most immediately under discussion. The small question goes to the heart of the matter.

Protagoras is asked to choose between the oneness of homogeneity, where different names refer to smaller or larger por-

---

16. 324d7–8: πότερον ἔστι τι ἕν. At 324e3: τὸ ἕν. At 325a2: συλλήβδην ἓν αὐτὸ . . . ἀνδρὸς ἀρετήν.

tions of the same thing (as different parts of a lump of gold), and the oneness of heterogeneity, where the components differ from each other but together make up a single whole (as the parts of a face). Protagoras, committed as he is to *some* sort of unity, asserts that the virtues "are in the relation of the parts of a face to the whole" (329d8–e2). Yet the little he says makes it doubtful that, in his view, the virtues even possess the unity of heterogeneity. "Many men are brave but unjust, and others are just but not wise" (329e5–6), but presumably, to the degree to which they *are* brave or just, they are virtuous. But a nose without ears and eyes is not a face at all, so that on the analogy of a face, a man who is *only* brave or *only* just would not be virtuous. Gomperz correctly remarks that Protagoras "takes his stand on the common judgment which knows nothing of that unity of all virtues."[17]

The small question uncovers the central tension in the way of Protagoras. Protagoras chooses to have no doctrine of virtue of his own, but accepts without questioning the conventional morality current in his pupils' societies. At the same time, the Sophist professes to teach a subject matter, and this calls at the least for synthesis and generalization. That process, in turn, is not simply a matter of toting up particulars: the assumptions that underlie conventional morality must be made explicit. Thus, when in the course of such investigations contradictions are uncovered (and nothing guarantees that ordinary morality is free of them), a point of choice is reached which requires the use of a criterion that cannot itself be merely a commonly held belief. The push toward assumptions is tantamount to a push toward theory. This is the burden of the succession of arguments Socrates now propounds.

Protagoras maintains that the virtues "differ both in themselves and in their functions" (330b1–3) and that no one resembles any other. Socrates begins his challenge of this thesis

---

17. Theodor Gomperz, *Greek Thinkers,* trans. G. G. Berry (London: John Murray, 1905), II, 313.

by proposing to establish that justice resembles holiness. Formulated schematically, this argument may be stated as follows:

> *1.01.* Justice is a thing (330b–c).
> *1.02.* Justice is just (rather than unjust) (330c).
> *1.03.* Thus justice is of a class to be just (330c).

Similarly,

> *1.04.* Holiness is a thing (330d).
> *1.05.* Holiness is holy (for nothing could be holy, if holiness were not) (330e).
> *1.06.* Thus holiness is of a class to be holy (330d).

Now,

> *1.07.* Holiness is not unjust (331a).[18]
> *1.08.* Thus holiness is not not-just (331a).
> *1.09.* Therefore holiness is just (331a).

At the same time,

> *1.10.* Justice is not unholy (331a).
> *1.11.* Thus justice is not not-holy (331a).
> *1.12.* Therefore justice is holy (331a).

While Socrates concludes *1.09* and *1.12* in his own behalf, he concludes in behalf of Protagoras that

> *1.13.* Justice is either the same as holiness or it is very like it.

"And above all,"

> *1.14.* Justice is of the same class as holiness (331b).

---

18. *1.07–1.12* does not give the argument as Socrates formulates it. Rather, he reminds Protagoras, after *1.06,* that in the Sophist's view the virtues do *not* resemble one another and then draws from this the *unacceptable* conclusion that holiness is unjust and justice unholy (331a). Socrates' inferences are clearer when his argument is formulated as positively supporting the conclusion he proposes to maintain.

Protagoras immediately expresses his unwillingness to grant the conclusion Socrates draws for himself (the conjunction of *1.09* and *1.12*), insisting that there is a difference between the two virtues. He thus also rejects a part of the conclusion Socrates states in his partner's behalf, namely that which identifies justice and holiness (*1.13*). Yet this rejection is nonetheless compatible with the claim that the two virtues resemble each other (*1.14*); indeed, in a grudging and unhelpful way, Protagoras yields on this point a moment later. But before we are ready to take up Protagoras' response, Socrates' much disputed argument calls for extensive comment.

SELF-PREDICATION. Justice is not just and holiness is not holy, any more than redness is red.[19] We would not hesitate to say so if "justice" and "holiness" were the names of universals. But when Socrates asks Protagoras to agree that justice and holiness are things (the word is *prâgma*), he does not have simple universals in mind. At the time the *Protagoras* was written, Plato was beginning to develop what has come to be called his "theory" of forms.[20] The forms, as they appear explicitly, above all in the *Phaedo* and the *Republic,* come to be a part of Plato's conceptual arsenal in response to several related philosophic perplexities. In the first instance, he felt a need to give philosophic support to Socrates'—and his own—quests for definitions of key ethical as well as metaphysical concepts. As their denotata, the forms play a role in Plato's theory of meaning. But the forms also have metaphysical and normative functions: they constitute answers to questions about the causes of things and they are models of perfection which serve as the measure of the imperfect particulars of the empirical world. For a long period in Plato's career, the forms were *used* as answers to questions in the way in which hammers and saws are used by the carpenter. Not until the much later

19. As Gomperz points out so vehemently in *Greek Thinkers*, II, 313.
20. What follows is an undocumented summary of what is argued in some detail in Ch. 3, especially Secs. II, X, and XI.

Parmenides does Plato raise questions about the theory of forms itself, as a toolmaker might reflect on the various characteristics of the implements he makes. Only *then* does Plato indicate that he sees a fatal tension among the diverse functions that he has his forms fulfill.

Given such a development over a long stretch of time, the forms, as they appear in a dialogue as early as the *Protagoras*, must be thought of as conceived in an inchoate way, with only those of their features in conscious focus which are directly relevant to a given context. We know—again especially from the *Phaedo* and the *Republic*—that forms come to function as paradigms, as the perfect exemplars of beauty or equality or justice, which are only imperfectly embodied in the world of becoming. And such models *do* possess the characteristics of which they are the paradigms: absolute beauty *is* beautiful, perfect equality *is* equal, and paradigmatic justice *is* just. Precisely that which is imperfect in the world as we encounter it —the beauty of a poem, the equality of two stones, the justice of a ruler's action—exists perfectly in the form.

When Socrates first insists that both justice and holiness are things and emphatically rejects that they might be unjust and unholy respectively, we know that he has begun to think of paradigms. For justice cannot be unjust for the very same reason that a perfect diamond cannot embody any of the flaws that diamonds are capable of possessing. Socrates' point is not the logical one he might make if he wanted to maintain that the *universal,* red, cannot be blue, on the grounds that no color at all is predicable of any universal whatsoever. That he is not talking logic is clearer still when Socrates comes to holiness. The very question as to whether holiness is holy is rejected, and he insists that "nothing else could well be holy if we won't allow holiness itself to be so" (330d8–e1). This sentence is intelligible only if holiness is taken to be the perfectly holy thing and the measure of all familiar instances of that virtue.

Socrates makes no attempt to fool Protagoras by insisting that justice is just and holiness is holy. These initial premises emerge naturally out of Plato's developing reflections and are seriously intended. We must not permit this fact to be obscured because *we* are disinclined to allow self-predicative paradigms or even because Plato himself later came to have reservations about such a conception of forms.[21] At the beginning of his argument (that is, *1.02* and *1.05*), Socrates employs premises his creator thought to be true.

UNJUST AND NON-JUST. While the first and second major problems raised in the argument under discussion are connected, that of self-predication stems from an issue that comes into focus only after the *Protagoras* was written. The controversial move from "holiness is not unjust" (*1.07*) to "holiness is not not-just" (*1.08*) and thus to "holiness is just" (*1.09*)—as well as the inference from *1.10* to *1.11* and *1.12*—touches on the central theme of the *Protagoras*. I want first to consider the inferences Socrates makes here and only subsequently to take up the merit of the premises themselves.

We are not simply concerned with the formal properties of this inference, or we could make short shrift of it. From (*i*) "*x* is not un-*F*" one cannot get (*ii*) "*x* is not not-*F*," because "un" and "not" simply do not have the same meaning. For example, *i* may be true by virtue of the fact that *x* is the *sort* of thing of which neither "*F*" nor "un-*F*" can meaningfully be predicated. Stones are not unhappy (meaning "it is not the case that stones are unhappy"); we do not wish to be entitled to infer from this that stones are not not-happy ("it is not the case that stones are not-happy") and thus that they are happy.

Plato's Socrates is not doing exercises in formal logic. The issue is not whether the inference is possible for *any x* and *any F*, but whether one is justified in making it when the subjects are "justice" and "holiness" and the predicates are "just" and "holy." And here we must remember that holiness and justice are regarded as perfect models of what is holy or just, so that

---

21. In Ch. 3, I argue that in the *Parmenides* Plato gives expression to such reservations. See especially Secs. V and VI.

holiness, for example, is the sort of thing that at least *might* be just or unjust. In short, for the cases *we* are interested in, it is not the case that *i* is true—if it is true at all—simply because *neither F nor* un-*F* is properly predicated of the subject.

This last observation, however, by no means warrants the inference from "holiness is not unjust" to "holiness is just." Perhaps holiness is not unjust because it is *neutral* with respect to justice and injustice, so that it is not just either. Consider Jane, who lives down the street. She may very well not be ugly (as Medusa is), but, unfortunately for her, it does not follow that, like Helen of Troy, she is beautiful. Jane's face may merely be plain, so that it would be false to say of her that she is only a little beautiful (as lukewarm water is just a little hot) or slightly ugly (as cool water is only somewhat cold).

Suppose, now, that the opposite is true for "just" and "holy"; suppose that nothing of which "just" and "holy" can ever meaningfully be predicated—such as human acts and human characters—fails to be just or holy or unjust or unholy at least to some degree; suppose that no acts or characters are ever *neutral* with respect to either of these pairs of traits. If that were so, it would make good sense to say that if some given act or character is less just or holy than are some alternatives to it, that given act or character is simply unjust or unholy (without at all assuming that because an act or a man is not perfectly just or holy, it or he is perfectly unjust or unholy).

Before we return to the paradigms of justice and holiness themselves, it must thus be recognized that the legitimacy of Socrates' inferences—and it still is the inference that concerns us, not the truth of the premises—rests on the thesis that no human act or human character (and whatever else is of the sort that might be just or holy) is ever neutral with respect to justice and injustice, holiness and unholiness. And however sparse and indirect the evidence may be, there is no doubt that Plato's Socrates holds this view. Socrates would be unwilling, to put the point negatively, to call any human act or character

simply non-just or non-holy and to say that neither of these
predicates or their opposites apply.

The evidence *is* sparse and indirect, although this fact itself
is of importance to an understanding of the *Protagoras*. In that
dialogue, only the art of measurement which Socrates later
sketches out can be introduced as relevant. Socrates there
maintains that it is possible to devise a science of conduct that
will enable men to make correct choices in life.[22] Decisions
as to what one ought to do are to be based on knowledge and,
if made in accordance with the method recommended, will be
rational. But the very possibility of such rationality in conduct
depends upon a world in which the alternatives that are open
to men cannot be morally neutral. For neutrality spells arbi-
trariness; it means the possibility of choice to which a science
of measurement cannot apply.

The *Republic* provides additional, if even less direct, support. The components of the human psyche mind their own
business more or less well, so that a man is always more or less
just or unjust. It is not possible to be human and yet possess
a character that falls outside the sphere of morality. All men,
from the philosopher to the tyrant, are to be measured on the
scale of justice.[23] And going still further afield, one might note
that a universe in which the Good plays the role of the sun can
hardly be one in which a Humean distinction is possible between fact and value; it cannot be a world which leaves room
for moral vacuums.

This doctrine is so pervasive in Plato's thought that it is hard
to imagine him creating a Socrates whose views are incompatible with it. One might indeed be tempted to explain the lack
of evidence, in the *Protagoras,* for the thesis that whatever sort
of thing is capable of being just, etc., *is* to some degree just or
unjust, etc. by claiming that Plato took it so much for granted
that he never felt the need to spell it out and to support it. But

---

22. For a discussion of this entire passage, see Sec. IX.
23. *Republic* 441c–444e, 543a–576b.

this view fails to take account of the presence of Protagoras and of the structure of the dialogue.

Socrates' argument here depends upon a premise which insists on the ubiquity of morality. Protagoras, on the other hand, the spokesman for conventional morality, cannot be regarded as subscribing to the same assumption. No doubt he holds the common sense view that there are large areas of human conduct which are neither just nor unjust, neither holy nor unholy. If so fundamental a disagreement were made explicit—and so early in the dialogue, moreover—by having Socrates put his assumption on the table, the purpose of the entire work would be deflected.

The *Protagoras* seeks to exhibit dramatically two modes of life informed by two distinct conceptions of morality and to show them in conflict with each other. It does not propose to *establish* one or another thesis. This drama does call, as we shall see, for a progressive revelation of substantive moral assumptions: Socrates begins with arguments that appear to be purely formal in character and goes on to show more of his own hand and to show up more of Protagoras'. If Plato were to start out, however, by having Socrates come into the open on an issue of this magnitude, he would be introducing a topic that calls for treatment on the scale of the *Republic*. To make explicit Socrates' premise here and to argue for it would require Plato to write a dialogue very different from the *Protagoras* he set out to write.

For Socrates, it is permissible to infer that if one human act is less just than some other, then that act is unjust. If it remains unclear why this should be allowed, the legitimacy of the inference may be more manifest when the subjects of these moral predicates are not acts or characters, but the paradigms of justice and holiness. If the exemplar of justice is holy at all —and we are still not concerned with the truth of this—then it must be perfectly holy. What sense would it make to say that a paradigm possesses characteristics in precisely the imperfect way as do human beings who are subject to all the

vicissitudes of the world of becoming?[24] The absence of
moral neutrality among perfect entities calls for the perfect
possession of moral traits and rules out all intermediaries. If
holiness is not unjust and not merely non-just either, what else
could it be but just and perfectly so? Given, then, the self-
predicative nature of paradigms and a world that does not
allow for moral neutrality, the controversial inferences that
yield the conclusions that holiness is just and justice is holy are
warranted.

We are finally ready to consider the truth of the premises
that holiness is not unjust (*1.07*) and that justice is not unholy
(*1.10*). A world can be imagined in which it is possible for a
holy act to be unjust and a just act unholy. Suppose that holiness requires one to do what god commands and justice calls
for our giving every man his due: it is then perfectly possible
to conceive of a god and a world so constituted that the demands of holiness and justice always conflict. So harsh a god
would then be calling on men to choose, in every case, between
him and their fellow creatures; men could thus either serve god
or other men, but never both.

If neutrality with respect to moral characteristics is eliminated, one would have to envisage precisely so extreme a view
if one wished to deny the truth of Socrates' premises. But
surely Plato's Socrates could not subscribe to such a view of
the relation between holiness and justice. Man and the world
are so constituted that it is possible to lead a good life, however difficult it may be to achieve it. Neither Plato nor Protagoras, for that matter, would have understood a notion such
as that of original sin. Each in his own way thought that the
world presented obstacles to the good life; each thought that
great effort was required if such a life was to be achieved or

---

24. There are, of course, problems here if one wants to spell out a
coherent *theory* of such paradigms. But these difficulties pertain to the
self-predicative character of the paradigms of which Plato became aware
only when he set out to write the *Parmenides*. See the discussion in Ch. 3
already referred to.

even approximated; but neither of them held that the world was so morally flawed that such a life was impossible—or possible only through miraculous intervention, such as by grace. In short, there is nothing in the views of either Socrates or Protagoras to suggest that they might have been tempted to deny the compatibility of holiness and justice. We should thus not be surprised at all to have Socrates claim, without apology or explanation, that holiness is not unjust nor justice unholy.[25]

At last we can look at the array of conclusions Socrates draws from his argument and at Protagoras' response to them. In his own behalf, Socrates concludes that justice is holy and holiness just (*1.09* and *1.12*). This is, so to speak, the bare logical result of the argument. But if one is to understand just how the issue of the heterogeneity of the virtues is affected by it, further interpretation is called for. Accordingly, Socrates goes on to draw conclusions in Protagoras' behalf. First, a strong one which he does not insist upon: justice is the same as holiness or extremely like it (*1.13*); and next, a weaker one about which he has no doubts: justice is of the same class as holiness (*1.14*).[26] At the very least, that is, these virtues are homogeneous.

Socrates himself is not at ease with the strong conclusion. Not only does he not demand that Protagoras accept it, but he states it in what can only be called a wobbly way: there is much difference between identity and even the greatest of similarities. Yet this uncertainty is not difficult to understand, given that at the time of the writing of the *Protagoras* Plato

---

25. Socrates' amazement that for the sake of holiness, Euthyphro should propose to prosecute his father reflects this unwillingness to believe that the command of the gods could be incompatible with the obligations men have to each other. See *Euthyphro* 3e–4e; the entire dialogue can be read as supportive of what is here maintained about the relation between justice and holiness.

26. Note that this conclusion is reached with the aid of premises *1.03* and *1.06*.

had by no means worked out a doctrine of paradigmatic forms. For premises drawn from such a doctrine are needed to show the identity of the two virtues.[27] In his first conclusion, then, Socrates gives expression to a metaphysical *insight:* he sees, if not too clearly, that what he has said up to this point implies some extremely close relation between justice and holiness, possibly their identity. Accordingly, it is not only irrelevant to the purpose of the dialogue to show why justice and holiness are identical, but Plato is in no position to do so and hence Socrates cannot insist upon it.

If the two virtues were identical, the matter of their homogeneity would *a fortiori* be settled.[28] But Plato could hardly have portrayed a Protagoras who was ready to follow the leap that was made to reach this conclusion. Thus Socrates also offers a second interpretation of *1.09* and *1.12,* which in effect claims *only* that justice and holiness are homogeneous. On this Socrates insists, while Protagoras balks.

More specifically, Protagoras begins his objection earlier than that. "I can't really admit that justice is holy and holiness just" (331b8–c2), he says, right away following this by the first indication of his attitude toward the kind of strenuous dialectic inquiry in which Socrates engages him: "however, . . . what does it matter? If you like, let us assume that justice is holy and holiness just" (331c3–4). Protagoras thus immediately drops his initial objection and proceeds to question Socrates' claim that justice and holiness are homogeneous. "After all, everything resembles everything else up to a point. There

---

27. An argument might be sketched out as follows. If the form of justice is holy, it must be perfectly so, and if the form of holiness is just, it must be perfectly just. Thus each of the "two" forms is an exemplar of both justice and holiness. But as paradigms, there is nothing other than that of which they are the paradigms which can distinguish them, so that the forms of justice and of holiness must be the same form. The two virtues are thus one.

28. See pp. 86–88 of the useful article by David Gallop, "Justice and Holiness in *Protagoras* 330–331," *Phronesis,* 6 (1961).

is a sense in which white resembles black, and hard soft"
(331d2–4), he says, and goes on to complain of Socrates' procedure. "By your method you can prove, if you want to, that
[even the parts of the face] too all resemble one another. But
it is not right to call things similar because they have some one
point of similarity, even when the resemblance is very slight"
(331d8–e4).

In no way does Protagoras here do justice to the argument
Socrates has made.[29] To begin with, Socrates does *not* rest his
claim that justice and holiness belong to the same class on the
discovery of the ubiquity of some adventitious resemblance
between any given thing and everything else. Protagoras ignores the fact that the argument is specifically and solely concerned with the two virtues in question and fails to perceive
that it presupposes the substantive principle that no action is
morally neutral. Moreover, if it is true that holiness is just and
justice holy, the relation between the two virtues thus pointed
to is not some trivial similarity between them. Quite the contrary, the resemblance in question tells us a good deal about
the two traits considered *as virtues* and is immediately relevant to the central issue under discussion.[30] The dual claim
does justify the thesis that justice and holiness are homogeneous.

The sparring between Socrates and Protagoras has only begun, yet the first round is typical of others to come. On the one
hand, Socrates does not convince Protagoras of the conclusion
he derives, while, on the other, Protagoras fails to discover the
true nature of the argument that is directed against him. A
more telling objection to Socrates' demonstration would require an examination of the assumptions which underlie it; but

29. I sharply disagree with the thesis of Gallop's paper (*ibid.*), which
essentially supports this objection by Protagoras.

30. To note, by contrast, that squirrels are gray and that elephants are
gray tells us nothing about the similarity of these two species *as animals*.

Protagoras is not prepared to take this step toward philosophy. However, as the dialogue progresses, the pressure from Socrates will mount.

V. WISDOM AND TEMPERANCE (332a–333b)

Socrates wastes no words in response to Protagoras, but proceeds without pause to present an argument in support of the conclusion that "temperance and wisdom must be the same" (333b4–5).[31] The argument falls into two parts, of which the first aims to show that "foolish behavior is the opposite of temperate" (332b3–4), while the second uses that premise in an attempt to force Protagoras to agree that temperance and wisdom are the same. It will be convenient to begin with the latter part without questioning its opening premise.

> *2.05.* Foolish acts are the opposite of temperate acts (332b).
>
> *2.06.* Foolish acts are a function of folly (332b).
>
> *2.07.* Temperate acts are a function of temperance (332b).
>
> *2.08.* Any act of a certain kind is a function of a faculty of that kind (332c).[32]
>
> *2.09.* Any act that is the opposite of a certain kind is a function of a faculty of the opposite of that kind (332c).[32]
>
> *2.10.* Anything that has an opposite has only one opposite (332d).[33]

From this it is concluded—and Socrates twice reiterates each of his premises—that

---

31. Socrates' reasoning in this passage has been widely criticized. See especially the discussion in *Vlastos, 1956,* pp. xxviii–xxxi. The aim of the present essay is to take another look at this and the other arguments as parts of a larger whole.

32. Based on the examples of strength, weakness, swiftness, and slowness.

33. Based on the examples of beautiful-ugly, good-evil, high pitch-low pitch.

2.11. Folly is the opposite of temperance (332e).

Earlier, however, it was agreed that

2.12. Folly is the opposite of wisdom (332e),

so that

2.13. It cannot be the case both that "wisdom is different from temperance" and that (*2.10*) "anything that has an opposite has only one opposite" (333a).

But since *2.10* cannot be rejected, it follows that

2.14. Temperance and wisdom are the same (333b).

Two more virtues are identified.

If, for the moment, we leave "opposite" uninterpreted, no special problems are raised by the progress from *2.05* to *2.11*. It has been strenuously objected, however, that Socrates does not offer Protagoras the option of rejecting one of the *four* propositions that were required to reach the final conclusion.[34] Socrates knows full well that *2.10* cannot be rejected (the very meaning of "opposite" implies its truth); and besides this dictum, he allows his opponent to give up only his own (that is, Protagoras') claim: that wisdom and temperance are different. In short, Protagoras is given no opportunity to reject either that folly is the opposite of temperance (*2.11*) or that folly is the opposite of wisdom (*2.12*), although both of them are needed for Socrates' conclusion.[35]

Yet why should Socrates proceed in so textbookish a fashion? The second of the missing propositions is a matter of common sense: if wisdom has any opposite at all, surely it is folly; no one is expected to deny this. That folly should also be the opposite of temperance, on the other hand, is not at all

---

34. *Vlastos, 1956,* pp. xxviii–xxix.
35. Given Vlastos' strongly worded objection to the procedure Socrates uses here (*ibid.*), it is worth pointing out that Socrates reiterates each of the disjuncts separately (333a–b) and thus makes the basis of his argument fully explicit.

obvious, and one might well be strongly inclined to reject it. But then this is precisely the premise—and the only one—for which Socrates has given a supporting argument. Only a moment earlier he forced Protagoras to agree to it, by means of a series of steps (*2.05–2.10*) that were presented as entailing that controversial claim. In sharp contrast to this, Protagoras nowhere supports his own view that temperance and wisdom are different; all we have are his dogmatic statements to the effect that the virtues are heterogeneous. In this way, the manner of the argument exhibits one of Plato's aims in the dialogue: an opinion that is merely asserted (the way of Protagoras) must yield to one that is the product of inquiry (the way of Socrates).

While Socrates' general way of proceeding is thus perfectly proper, it certainly does not follow that the controversial step in his argument—that folly is the opposite of temperance—must also be accepted. It is immediately obvious that the crucial premise in the argument that is meant to establish it is (*2.05*), "foolish acts are the opposite of temperate acts," so that the major burden of the refutation of Protagoras' belief in the heterogeneity of wisdom and temperance rests on Socrates' success in showing that premise to be true.[36]

Three premises are quickly asserted and agreed to.

2.01. All right (and useful[37]) acts are temperate (332a).

---

36. In what follows I am greatly indebted to two papers devoted to this argument. The first, by David Savan—"Socrates' Logic and the Unity of Wisdom and Temperance," in R. J. Butler (ed.), *Analytical Philosophy: Second Series* (Oxford: Blackwell, 1965)—seeks to show that Socrates successfully establishes that foolish acts are the opposite of temperate acts, and the second, by David Gauthier—"The Unity of Wisdom and Temperance," *Phronesis*, 6 (1968)—argues that the Savan defense is unsuccessful. While I find myself in agreement with the conclusions of neither of these essays, both of them greatly advance the understanding of Socrates' argument, particularly the original Savan paper.

37. No further reference is made in the argument to this "useful." $\dot{o}\rho\theta\hat{\omega}s$ $\tau\epsilon$ $\kappa\alpha\grave{\iota}$ $\dot{\omega}\phi\epsilon\lambda\acute{\iota}\mu\omega s$ (332a6–7) might thus be read as "rightly, *that is*, usefully" and Socrates interpreted as not wishing to differentiate between the two. But also see n. 88, p. 116, below.

2.02. All wrong acts are foolish (332b).

2.03. All foolish acts are not temperate (332b).

Then, without objection from Protagoras, Socrates draws the conclusion that

2.05. Foolish acts are the opposite of temperate acts (332b).

Clearly, *2.05* does not follow from the premises as they stand.[38] At the very least, a further assumption, to the effect that

2.04. Right acts are the opposite of wrong acts

is required. No difficulties are raised by the fact that this premise remains suppressed, for its truth is just as evident as that folly is the opposite of wisdom, an assertion that was readily agreed upon at the outset of the argument (332a).

But even now, when *2.04* is supplied, the deduction of the controversial *2.05* cannot be adequately evaluated, nor can the argument as a whole be properly assessed. An interpretation is still needed of the relation ". . . is the opposite of . . .," which makes a crucial appearance in *2.04* and *2.05*, as well as in *2.09–2.12*.

On at least one understanding of oppositeness, the argument—with the suppressed premise supplied—is clearly valid.[39] If "right" and "wrong" were contradictories in the way "odd" and "even" are, "foolish" and "temperate" would also be shown to be a contradictory pair. On this interpretation of "opposite," a predicate F is the opposite of G when the following is true: if anything is F, it is not G *and* if it is G, it is not F *and* (assuming F and G can be meaningfully predicated of it) if it is not F, it is G and if it is not G, it is F.[40] If *2.01–2.05* are

---

38. As Vlastos shows, it certainly does not follow from *2.03* alone (*Vlastos, 1956*, p. xxix, n. 19). But then there is no reason to suppose that it was meant to, since this would leave no function at all for *2.01* and *2.02*.

39. I wish here to reiterate my dependence on the Savan and Gauthier papers earlier referred to. To spell out in detail how my account differs from either of theirs would, however, take us too far afield.

40. "F is the contradictory of G" is thus defined as "$F \equiv \sim G$."

then rewritten so as to express this conception of oppositeness, the validity of the argument readily becomes apparent

> *2.01'.* If an act is right, it is temperate.
> *2.02'.* If an act is wrong, it is foolish.
> *2.03'.* If an act is foolish, it is not temperate.
> *2.04'.* An act is right if, and only if, it is not wrong.
> *2.05'.* Therefore, an act is foolish if, and only if, it is not temperate.[41]

Given this result and provisionally taking wisdom and folly also to be contradictories, Socrates' final conclusion also follows. The dictum about opposites (which, on this intrepretation should now be reformulated to read, "any predicate that has a contradictory has only one contradictory") need no longer appear as a premise, for it has been incorporated into the very formulation of the different sets of opposites. Thus from

> *2.05'.* An act is foolish if, and only if, it is not temperate,

together with *2.06–2.09,* we get

> *2.11'.* A man has the faculty of foolishness if, and only if, he does not have the faculty of temperance,

which, with a rewritten version of *2.12,*

> *2.12'.* A man has the faculty of foolishness if, and only if, he does not possess the faculty of wisdom,

finally yields the conclusion:

> *2.14'.* A man has the faculty of temperance if, and only if, he has the faculty of wisdom.[42]

---

41. This may be formulated as follows:
$R \supset T; Wr \supset F; F \supset \sim T; R \equiv \sim Wr; \therefore F \equiv \sim T.$

42. Ignoring Socrates' concern with the "faculties" of foolishness, temperance, etc., this comes to:
$F \equiv \sim T; F \equiv \sim Wi; \therefore T \equiv Wi.$

If "right" and "wrong" and "wise" and "foolish" were like "odd" and "even" (or at least thought to be by the protagonists of our dialogue), we could now declare the argument to be valid, turn to consider the truth of some of its steps, and attend to its place in the *Protagoras* as a whole. But clearly, there is a difference between the two pairs of predicates with which we are concerned and the opposition of a pair that brooks no intermediates. Both wisdom and rightness (as well as their opposites) are subject to degree: Protagoras claims to make men a little wiser every day, and surely some men are capable of acting more virtuously than others.[43]

Intermediates to be found between two extremes can, however, be of at least two sorts. They might, like plain Jane who is neither beautiful nor ugly, be simply neutral with respect to the scale that has Helen at one limit and Medusa at the other. Such opposites are contraries in the sense in which Savan identifies them[44] and for which no extensional analysis analogous to that given for contradictoriness is possible.[45] Accordingly, if the opposites, "wise" and "foolish," "right" and "wrong," were taken to be in this sense contraries, there would be no way of testing for the validity of the argument.

But while the two pairs of opposites with which we are here concerned are not contradictories like "odd" and "even," neither is there, at least for Plato's Socrates, a neutral stretch be-

---

43. I agree with Savan that "wisdom" and "folly" are not contradictories on the order of "odd" and "even," but disagree with him that Protagoras holds "right" and "wrong" to be in this way contradictories ("Socrates' Logic," in Butler, *Analytical Philosophy*, pp. 22, 24–25). Unlike Savan, I take Protagoras' distinction between savages and civilized men (before Hermes versus after him: two states between which there can *not* be an intermediate stage) to be equivalent to the conditions of amorality and morality. Right and wrong have a place *within* the city and there (as Savan agrees) they are subject to degree.

44. *Ibid.*, p. 21.

45. This is pointed out by Gauthier ("The Unity of Wisdom and Temperance," p. 159). While contrary predicates, F and G, are incompatible, we cannot assert $F \equiv \sim G$, since a thing of which F and G can meaningfully be predicated might nonetheless be *neither F nor G*.

tween perfect wisdom and abysmal folly or between the perfectly right and the utterly wrong.[46] Every act is to some degree wise (or foolish) and right (or wrong) and the faculties—that is, the states of character—from which such acts issue forth are similarly to be located *on* the lines that run from one extreme to the other: no person is simply non-wise and no one who is human (that is, touched by Hermes) is amoral.

These facts make every difference to the intelligibility of Socrates' argument. We do not need to decide where the line between wisdom and folly, between right and wrong, should be drawn. Perhaps only perfection merits the designation "wise" or "right"; or, following Simonides, perhaps all but the utterly foolish and wrong deserve to be so called.[47] Moreover, no fixed point need divide the continuum into a plus and a minus section; instead, one can, for any two alternatives, regard the wiser or more right as wise or right and the other as foolish or wrong. However that may be—and the *Protagoras* does not provide evidence for a decision—the predicates that are said by Socrates to be standing in opposition to each other must be treated as contradictories. If one applies, the other does not; and if one does not apply, the other does. While the predicates with which we are concerned are not like "odd" or "even," Socrates reaches his conclusion by means of the valid argument earlier set forth.[48]

---

46. On essentially the same evidence as was given for "justice" in Sec. IV. See pp. 73–77, above.

47. *To me that man suffices*
   Who is not bad or overweak, but sound
   In heart and knowing righteousness, the weal
   Of nations. I shall find no fault with him—(346c).

48. There *is* a paucity of evidence as to just how the predicates of this argument are opposed to each other; indeed, it remains entirely possible that the way in which wisdom and folly, etc., are opposite each other is simply unanalyzed in Plato's mind. While this fact—if it is one—would seriously affect one's position on the argument's validity, it would be much less relevant to the question of Plato's *intention* in having Socrates put

Although Plato almost certainly thought the argument against Protagoras to be valid, he surely did not think that his Socrates had actually demonstrated the identity of wisdom and temperance. The argument goes along at breakneck speed: a confident and insistent Socrates imposes his skill on a reluctant and confused Protagoras. Not a moment is allotted to reflection. (Socrates does not even bother to wait for Protagoras' assent to the final conclusion, but immediately moves on to his next argument.) Thus a tension is created between the argument's brisk competence and its profound unsatisfactoriness as a support of its conclusion—a tension that expresses what I believe to be this passage's major role in the dialogue.

For the most part, the argument proceeds on the loftiest plane of formality. The moral concepts that figure in it are hardly treated as such, but are largely dealt with as if they were variables possessing only a few logical properties. X's are y's and y's are the opposite of z's and before you know it, there is no difference between *sophrôsyne* and *sophia*. An important moral thesis is "established"—not through the investigation of the moral issues that underlie it, but by means of the most arid dialectic. By controverting Protagoras' claim concerning the heterogeneity of the virtues in a way that is at once logically powerful and philosophically unsatisfactory, Socrates demonstrates to his partner in discussion the necessity of philosophy.

Only the first three premises (*2.01–2.03*) have any moral content of interest and all three can be seen as emerging out of the morality which Protagoras defends. That all right (and useful) acts are temperate (*2.01*) constitutes a pious avowal of the importance of the virtue of temperance. To understand

---

forth this argument. Since the argument *is* valid if opposition is taken to be unqualified contradictoriness and since Plato had none of the machinery we use in analyzing logical connectives, there is every reason to think that Plato *thought* Socrates' argument to be valid, whatever may *actually* be the case.

why Protagoras assents to this proposition one need only imagine the storm of words that a denial would have provoked: "Are you not ashamed, Protagoras, teacher of virtue, to believe that it is possible to act in ways that are right and advantageous but not temperate?" Protagoras would surely not wish to claim that right acts might be *in*temperate, leaving only the possibility that for some right acts, temperance is irrelevant. While Protagoras might indeed be tempted to assert this—for it is congenial to a view that regards each virtue as a sort of special skill—it does bring him into conflict with his earlier insistence that it is vital for all citizens to possess temperance (324d).[49] This alternative, then, would require Protagoras to work out a reconciliation between different aspects of his position, thus forcing him into philosophy via another route.

Again, Protagoras has no choice but to maintain that all wrong acts are foolish (*2.02*). And if, in addition, one recognizes that they are also disadvantageous to the actor, what could be more foolish than to act in ways that are contrary to one's own interest? Accordingly, Protagoras' agreement with this premise also emerges immediately out of the received opinion he proposes to defend.

The last of the three premises seems at first blush to be somewhat further removed from the conventional morality Protagoras makes his own; that all foolish acts are not temperate (*2.03*) is less obviously a Protagorean premise. Nevertheless, the Sophist is committed to this premise as well, for it follows readily from propositions which Protagoras must be prepared to maintain: that (*i*) all temperate acts are right (for an act that is admittedly virtuous cannot be wrong) and that (*ii*) all foolish acts are wrong (for wisdom is counted among the virtues and there is no question that foolishness is its opposite). If one now also grants the truism that (*iii*) all

---

49. Usefully noted by Savan, "Socrates' Logic," in Butler, *Analytical Philosophy*, p. 24.

right acts are not wrong, that foolish acts are not temperate follows as well.[50]

Socrates demonstrates by means of a number of logical maneuvers that there are significant inconsistencies in Protagoras' position. Worse still, the very same dialectic can take propositions that have the ring of conventional good sense and derive from them a thesis that is far removed from the doctrine of the many. If the great Sophist is reluctant to admit that temperance and wisdom are the same, he shall have to undertake a serious inquiry into the very nature of the virtues.

VI. JUSTICE AND TEMPERANCE: THE ARGUMENT BREAKS DOWN (333b–338e)

The next argument remains incomplete—in itself it is barely longer than a page (333b–334c)—for Protagoras has come to the end of his patience. Yet this passage is of great importance, for it is the turning point of the dialogue and succinctly foreshadows major themes to be developed later.

Socrates, continuing his look at the relations holding among the virtues, two at a time, now asks whether an unjust man can be temperate in his injustice[51] and thus clearly reaches a moral issue of major significance.[52] Whether justice and holiness are identical or closely resemble each other is, after all, as much a question of theology as of moral theory; for whether or not they do, depends, before anything else, upon the will of

---

50. $T \supset R; F \supset Wr; R \supset \sim Wr; \therefore F \supset \sim T.$
51. 333d4. I here follow the revised Jowett translation in taking δοκοῦσί τινές σοι σωφρονεῖν ἀδικοῦντες as asking whether an unjust man *can* be temperate, rather than whether he *is*—that is, as raising a conceptual question and not just a factual one. B. Jowett (trans.), *The Dialogues of Plato* (4th ed., rev.; Oxford: Clarendon Press, 1953), I, 159.
52. This is also noted by Paul Friedlander in *Plato*, trans. Hans Meyerhoff ("Bollingen Series LIX" [New York: Pantheon Books, 1964]), II, 20.

the gods. Take temperance and wisdom; in the popular mind, they are at least closely allied. Perhaps the common view allows a wise man to be intemperate or a temperate man foolish, but the claim that these two virtues are identical does not constitute too great a wrench. The wise man surely is expected to be self-controlled and discretion is the better part of wisdom. The relation between justice and temperance, however, is another matter. Many men would insist that the two must be found together, that no one can be temperate in injustice. Yet at the same time, there is an "enlightened," "realistic," or "aristocratic" view which dismisses all such opinions as pious pap. Men may *talk* this way, this cynical position notes, but their actions suggest a very different view: the great success of some *un*just men can indeed be attributed precisely to their self-control, to their temperance.[53] There are thus two sharply divergent ways of understanding what the many believe regarding the relation of justice and temperance—one based on what they say, the other claiming an insight into what they do.

For Protagoras, furthermore, things are more complicated still. After all, he is engaged in a debate on the unity of the virtues. The "plebeian" view, which reacts with horror to the suggestion that injustice and temperance should be compatible, here plays into Socrates' hand. At the least, it suggests that a man is temperate, if and only if he is just. Yet the "enlightened" view is of no help to Protagoras' cause. According to it, temperance, a virtue, can be yoked to an end that is the very opposite of virtue: excellence can be put to the service of vice. This view suggests that the virtues are not heterogeneously unified, that they are not unified at all, that there is no "single whole, manly virtue" (325a2).

Socrates asks whether a man who acts unjustly can do so with temperance. And Protagoras at once responds "For my part I should be ashamed to agree to that. . . . Of course many

---

53. This is essentially the position Glaucon and Adeimantus want Socrates to refute in *Republic i.*

people do" (333c1-3). By taking this side, Protagoras tacitly gives in to Socrates' pressure toward regarding these virtues as equivalent. But for quite some time, neither of the disputants takes note of this fact,[54] for Socrates wishes nonetheless to inquire into the question and Protagoras agrees to answer in behalf of those holding the view opposite to his own. He will rue it: the logical tension to which he is subjected leads to an angry outburst of frustration.

From the thesis that "some people show temperance in doing wrong" (333d4), which Protagoras says he does *not* hold but is defending only to please Socrates, a number of consequences are quickly drawn. Temperance implies having good sense, so that men who are temperate, though unjust, can be said to plan well and hence be successful in doing wrong. Next Socrates proposes that some things are good, to wit those that are beneficial to man. The fat is in the fire; Protagoras explodes into a speech (to be returned to in a moment) from which the argument never recovers.

There is nothing obscure about the goal of Socrates' questioning. He is aiming at assent to two theses: that the good is what is beneficial for men and that success is precisely the achievement of that good. In this way, the incompatibility of temperance and injustice would become manifest, for one can surely not maintain that it is possible to achieve the good in doing wrong.

No doubt this is a powerful argument against the compatibility of injustice and temperance; but why should Protagoras become so angry when he glimpses the direction in which it is moving? Why not let Socrates finish and then calmly reply by saying "Thank you, Socrates, you have just shown that the position many people hold cannot sensibly be maintained. But

---

54. However, when the discussion of the unity of the virtues resumes, after the interlude on Simonides' poem, Protagoras concedes that there is a resemblance between justice and temperance as well as between justice and holiness and temperance and wisdom. See p. 103, below.

since my own view is the very opposite of theirs, you have happily shown mine to be correct"?

A deep inconsistency in his position prevents Protagoras from making this response. His initial answer to Socrates is consistent with this intention of upholding the morality of the many; yet the vehemence of his subsequent defense reveals that Protagoras also has a strong impulse to hold the very opposite view. Socrates' pressure uncovers an unresolvable conflict between two philosophic purposes of Protagoras. On the one hand, he aims merely to teach the morality of his pupils' society and does not lay claim to an ethic of his own which he would substitute for accepted custom. But on the other, his role as teacher is not fulfilled by retailing, one by one, the practices of Athens or whatever city. He uses reason to generalize and to push beneath the professions of the many to the beliefs underlying their actions. Add to this strain the issues raised by Protagoras' view on the unity of the virtues, and we need not be surprised that he explodes. Protagoras simply cannot do justice to all the demands he makes upon himself.

Protagoras' temper flares in the form of a speech. Things are not just good—period. Some are good on one occasion, harmful on another; what is good for one creature may, for another, be neither good nor bad; what is good in one sort of context need not be so when the context is different. The speech, replete with examples, insists on the total relativity of goodness. It functions to forestall the consideration of some single good-for-man, which Socrates was driving at, and it once again expresses the fact that Protagoras has no moral position of his own, which thus leaves the choice of goods to the society of his would-be pupils.

Yet it is not the substance of Protagoras' speech that leads to the breakdown, but the manner of it. The second major theme brought into focus by this brief argument fragment is the nature and function of discussion.

The audience applauds the speech; Socrates pleads a short

memory and asks Protagoras to keep his answers brief, so that he can hold on to the thread of the argument. Ostensibly, then, the wrangling that immediately ensues concerns the appropriateness of short and long answers.[55] And yet this is only the pretext for a debate about the way of the Philosopher versus that of the Sophist and an occasion for an exhibition of these roles acted out.

First Socrates and Protagoras both hold their ground: the former insists on short answers; the latter, a famous duelist with words, will not hand over the choice of weapons to his opponent (335a). The impasse allows Plato to sketch in the reactions of five leading members of the audience.

Callias takes Protagoras' side. A rich and powerful man, accustomed to command and to being obeyed, he physically prevents Socrates from leaving by grasping his hand and taking hold of his coat. He exercises his role as host—"We shan't let you go, Socrates. Our talk won't be the same without you" (335d2–3)—with a hint of violence. He fully accepts the combative conception of discussion by observing that "Protagoras is surely right in thinking that he is entitled to talk in the way that suits him, just as much as you are" (336b4–6).

Alcibiades then leaps into the ring as Socrates' second. He makes explicit what has been obvious all along, that it is not forgetfulness that makes Socrates want Protagoras to keep his answers short, but the evasiveness of Protagoras' long speeches. He too thinks of discussion as essentially a spectator sport (336b–d).

Next begins the attempt at mediation. Critias, the cultured amateur, simply announces the need for impartiality; Prodicus, however, makes distinctions. They must attend to the speakers impartially, not equally; the conversation must be a discussion, not a dispute; and while the speakers will be

---

55. The issue is brought up at 334c, 334e, 335b–c, 335e, 336a–b, and 338a.

esteemed and not praised, the hearers will derive enjoyment
rather than pleasure; and there are more distinctions still
(337a–c). Hippias finally reminds them all that they are the
best men of Greece assembled in the finest house in Athens—
We Happy Few!—and suggests that both Socrates and
Protagoras should yield a little on the length of the speeches
they consider appropriate. An arbitrator should be appointed
to enforce the middle way (337c–338b). The discussion is
from this point regarded less as a combat than as an entertainment for a self-selected elite. (No one suggests that the conversation should continue for the sake of arriving at the truth; no
one proposes that the discussion should take whatever form
will best achieve that end.)

Socrates makes short shrift of Hippias' simplistic solution,
in spite of the general applause it has evoked. It would be
wrong to appoint a referee of lesser ability than the disputants
and superfluous to designate one who is equal to them. But
none better than Protagoras is present (Socrates soothes the
ruffled feathers), leaving no one to whom the role of arbitrator
might be assigned. He suggests, instead, that for the sake of
the continuation of the discussion (though surely not of the inquiry), Protagoras should, for a while, assume the role of
questioner. Socrates, as respondent, will show how answers
should be given (338b–e).

The solution is accepted, though still reluctantly on
Protagoras' part. Just as in the dialogue as a whole, where
Socrates and Protagoras reverse positions, each defending the
view the other began with, so, in this middle section, Socrates
and Protagoras exchange the formal roles they have been playing. But just as the reversal of doctrines in the entire dialogue
is a matter of appearance only, so the reversal of roles now is
not in fact carried out. There is little questioning by
Protagoras and little answering by Socrates in the interpretation of the poem by Simonides, and Socrates most certainly
does not keep his speeches short.

VII. INTERPRETATION: THE POEM OF SIMONIDES (338e–349a)

This section is rich in humor and gives us a rest from the fatiguing duty of following complex arguments. In this way it prepares us for the final and most serious portion of the dialogue. The interpretation of Simonides' poem is perhaps the most elaborate example of "comic relief" in Plato's work. Nevertheless, it is not a digression, but advances the main theme of the dialogue. Early in the work, we saw Protagoras as the maker of an eloquent and persuasive speech. Now we shall see what sort of lesson Protagoras the teacher deems important. On the other side of this *Streit der Gelehrten,* we are treated to a Socratic critique in the form of a brilliant and revealing parody.

"In my view, Socrates, the most important part of a man's education is to become an authority on poetry. This means being able to criticize the good and bad points of a poem with understanding, to know how to distinguish them, and give one's reasons when asked" (338e6–339a3). So Protagoras begins when he takes over the discussion. For the traditional educator, the poets provide models of what is and is not excellent, as well as maxims that serve as guides for conduct. Moral wisdom is embedded in the work of Homer, Hesiod, Pindar, and others and, for the teachers of Greece, the task of harvesting that fruit consists in assimilating what the poets say. Protagoras proposes to bring reason to the problem of conduct, but still within the framework of received opinion. He stands midway between the traditionalists and the philosophers who are prepared to begin afresh by basing their ethical cogitations on an examination of man's nature and his good. Protagoras does not seek to replace the morality of the poets by his own: reason, for him, is limited to the function of generalizing and, above all, to a concern for logical consistency.

His critique of Simonides' poem, accordingly, is internal; he accuses the poet of contradicting himself.[56]

Simonides opens his poem with the assertion that "Hard is it on the one hand to become a good man truly" (339b1) and then goes on to criticize Pittacus, the sage, for claiming that "to be noble . . . is hard" (339c4–5). Protagoras triumphantly points out that assertion and criticism are incompatible. A familiar poem—everyone in the audience appears to know it—harbors a blatant inconsistency. Tradition has been given a brilliant jab. There is applause and Socrates feels giddy, as if "hit by a good boxer" (339e1–2).

With the one-page exposure of this fatal flaw in Simonides, Protagoras gives up the leadership of the discussion. He will regain it neither in the conversation about Simonides nor in the rest of the dialogue. Protagoras' interpretation has simply eliminated the poem: if the Sophist is right, reason has triumphed over Simonides and the job of interpretation is done. To be sure, one could now launch into a dialectical inquiry as to whether or not it *is* hard to be good, but this is not at all what Protagoras and his audience have in mind. Socrates and Protagoras are contestants locked in an entertaining battle of words. It is up to Socrates now to come to Simonides' defense, and he plays this role with gusto.

Invoking Homer and drawing upon Prodicus' linguistic skills, Socrates distinguishes between the tasks of *becoming* and *being* good: Simonides asserts the *former* to be difficult while criticizing Pittacus for thinking that the *latter* is hard. There is no contradiction (340a–d).

Prodicus is satisfied with this defense, but Protagoras is not. The poet cannot be so stupid as to think it easy to maintain virtue. Socrates now counters with a wild flurry of exegesis and traps poor Prodicus into supporting him. The specialist in

---

56. See the useful article by Leonard Woodbury, "Simonides on Arete," *Transactions and Proceedings of the American Philological Association*, 84 (1953); on the issue here taken up, pp. 137–138.

language—like Simonides, a native of Ceos—agrees that by *chalepon* the poet means not "hard" but "bad" and should be read as criticizing Pittacus for saying that it is *bad* to be noble (340e–341c). Protagoras, of course, will have none of this absurdity; and while Socrates immediately agrees that this reading is indeed not compatible with the next line, Prodicus has been embarrassed and the hazards of interpretation have been brought more sharply into focus. Still, Protagoras' charge of inconsistency remains standing.

Socrates meets the challenge by making a very long speech in which he turns to the rest of the poem for corroboration of his claim that Simonides distinguishes between becoming and being good. In a brilliantly humorous discourse, he first converts Simonides into a philosopher and then the poem into a philosophy.

Crete and Sparta—philosophers as well as Sophists have an ancient and mysterious provenance—harbored more men of wisdom than the rest of Greece. The athletic and warlike practices of Sparta were a cover for philosophical activity; it was lifted only when the citizenry expelled all foreigners once a year so as to be able to philosophize freely and in privacy. Not extensive discourse, but the fashioning of "pithy and memorable dicta" (343b2–3) was the method of this philosophy. (*Some* people, at least, were capable of giving short answers, though the humor here leaves no room for doubt that maxim-mongering stands at the other unphilosophic extreme from Protagoras' long-windedness.) The ancient sages admired this laconic brevity and Pittacus, in particular, gained fame from his dictum, "hard is it to be noble." Simonides was an ambitious philosopher and sought to make his career by flooring this well-known saying. He wrote the entire poem to vanquish Pittacus, the sage.

Having converted the least intellectual cities of Greece into centers of philosophy and Simonides the poet into a philosopher, Socrates is ready to transform the poem itself into a philosophic treatise. By means of a coherent doctrine, goes this interpretation, Simonides attacks the *bon mot* of Pittacus. The import of the outrageousness as well as the shrewdness of Socrates' fabulous account can be seen most readily when it is placed directly next to the poem itself.

The Poem of Simonides	Socrates' Commentary
1. *Hard is it on the one hand to become* 2. *A good man truly, hands and feet and mind* 3. *Foursquare, wrought without blame.* . . . . . .[57]	On the contrary, Pittacus, it is truly hard to become good, hands and feet, etc. "On the one hand" (*men*) must be read as a sign of a polemic against Pittacus and "truly" (*alâtheôs*) must be read as modifying "hard," rather than "good." Socrates clearly does violence to the text. (343c–344a)
4. *Nor do I count as sure the oft-quoted word* 5. *Of Pittacus, though wise indeed he was* 6. *Who spoke it. To be noble, said the sage, is hard.* 7. *A God alone can have this privilege.*	To *become* good, though it is hard, is possible; to *remain* a good man—which is what you, Pittacus, take to be hard—is impossible. Only a god has the privilege of remaining good. (344b–c)
8. *He cannot but be bad, whom once* 9. *Misfortune irredeemable casts down.*	Only he who *is* good cannot prevent himself from becoming bad in the event that misfortune should cast him down. (And only the resourceful—these are the good—can be cast down; the helpless—these are the bad—cannot be cast down; they already are.) The good may become bad; the bad are bad of necessity. For further support, Socrates quotes—at 344d7—from another poem: "The good

---

57. Seven lines here are presumed missing; they are believed to be the salutation to Scopas to whom the poem is addressed. See David A. Campbell, *Greek Lyric Poetry* (London: Macmillan; New York: St. Martin's Press, 1967), p. 386.

are sometimes bad and sometimes noble." (344c–e)

10. *For when he fares well every man is good,*
11. *But in ill-faring, evil.*

Whoever is good—and only he—can be made bad. On analogy with the crafts, becoming bad is always a matter of losing knowledge; e.g., a good doctor becomes bad by being deprived of his knowledge. Knowledge itself can be lost in several ways. (344e–345c)

12. *Then never shall I vainly cast away*
13. *In hopeless search my little share of life,*
14. *Seeking a thing impossible to be,*
15. *A man all blameless, among those who reap*
16. *The fruit of the broad earth. But should I find him*
17. *I'll send you word.*

Pittacus' claim that it is possible to be (i.e., remain) good is to be rejected emphatically. (Socrates here ignores the language of becoming: *to mê genesthai dunaton;* "what cannot come to be.") Therefore do not seek a completely blameless man.[58] (345c, 346d)

18. *But all who do no baseness willingly*
19. *I praise and love. The gods themselves strive not*
20. *Against necessity.*
21. *To me that man suffices*
22. *Who is not bad nor over-weak, but sound*
23. *In heart and knowing righteousness, the weal*
24. *Of nations. I shall find no fault with him—*
25. *For beyond number is the tribe of fools.*

I (Simonides) willingly praise and love those who do no baseness. ("Willingly" must be read as modifying Simonides' praising, for the poet surely did not believe that anyone could do evil voluntarily!) Those, that is, who are in a middle state regarding goodness, as distinguished from those who give praise under some sort of compulsion. (Socrates trades on Simonides' reputation as someone who would give praise for a fee.)[59] If I waited for a blameless person,

---

58. This is pointed out by Woodbury, "Simonides on Arete," pp. 146–147.

59. See, for example, Campbell, *Greek Lyric Poetry,* p. 379.

26. *All is fair that is unmixed with foul.*

I should never have anyone to praise. (Lines 19 and 20 are completely ignored.) If what you said, Pittacus, were even approximately right, I should not blame you. For I am no faultfinder (Socrates adds this line to the poem[60]); and if I were, there would be no shortage of objects worthy of censure. But since you made a completely false statement on an important subject, I must blame you. Nothing in this text has Simonides discussing the question of praising or blaming *Pittacus.* (345d–347a)

This, then, is how Socrates defends his claim that Simonides distinguishes between being and becoming good, criticizing Pittacus for thinking it hard to *be* good, while maintaining that it is only possible to *become* good. Hippias at once remarks that Socrates has given a fine exposition of the poem; but Plato certainly did not expect his readers to join Hippias in that belief. As in the etymology section of the *Cratylus,* there is here both brilliant sense and nonsense;[61] but the latter is too obvious to be missed. Socrates commits just about every sin of interpretation: (1) He puts words together that clearly do not belong together (lines 2, 18–19); (2) he ignores bits of text that would be difficult to harmonize with his thesis (lines 14, 19–20); (3) he puts in words that are no part of the poem (line 24) and even goes so far as to cite another poet for support (344d); (4) he does not hesitate to twist the text so as to have Simonides discuss a question regarding his own praising of Pittacus, rather than that of his praising men gen-

---

60. See Woodbury, "Simonides on Arete," p. 148.
61. See Ch. 1, Sec. V. This comparison is also made in Ulrich von Wilamowitz-Moellendorff, *Sappho und Simonides* (Berlin: Weidmannsche Buchhandlung, 1913), p. 167.

erally (lines 21–26); and, above all, (5) he imputes philosophic doctrines to Simonides of which there is no trace in the poem (lines 8–9, 10–11, 18–19).

Plato has provided us with a *reductio ad absurdum* of Protagoras' lesson. He has had Socrates bring in the entire poem, only to reveal more fully that he does not expect to achieve truth in this way—not about the difficulty of achieving virtue, nor even about the intentions of Simonides.[62] But in the course of Socrates' interpretation, he does something else as well: he completely changes the nature of Simonides' poem.

The man who addresses Scopas with some two dozen lines sums up his life experience as to the difficulty of achieving true virtue and points out that his view differs from that of a well-known sage. The poem epitomizes his observations of the world. There is little reasoning; there is no *doctrine* regarding the nature of virtuous action. Shamelessly, Socrates transforms all this. Goodness is always a matter of knowledge: only the knowing can be cast down. And to be cast down, to become bad, consists inevitably of a loss of that knowledge. This claim contains a far-from-ordinary conception of what it means to be virtuous; indeed, it constitutes a brief exposition of the very special Socratic doctrine which identifies virtue with knowledge. Simonides, as portrayed by Socrates, not only is a genuine philosopher, but anticipates the view Socrates comes to hold in this very dialogue. And so with the involuntary character of evil. Simonides believes—so Socrates assumes without

---

62. Hippias had applauded Socrates' account but nonetheless offered to provide his own. Presumably it would have been different had he been permitted to speak; presumably he would also have approved of *it*. Today, consult Wilamowitz, *Sappho und Simonides;* Hermann Gundert, "Die Simonides-Interpretation in Platons Protagoras," in *ERMHNEIA: Festschrift Otto Regenbogen* (Heidelberg: Carl Winter, 1952); and Woodbury, "Simonides on Arete," among others, for interpretations of the poem put forth by men who had far better intentions than Plato's Socrates. Although Simonides' poem is no more "difficult" than most, fundamental disagreements about it persist. Could Plato have been warning persons such as myself about interpreting the *Protagoras?*

a sign of hesitation—that men never do wrong willingly. Men cannot remain good, although this is always their intention, because they cannot always know what the good is. The difficulty of virtue is the difficulty of knowing. The impossibility of a sustained life of excellence is rooted in man's inability to have and to hold on to knowledge at every moment of his life.

Socrates' interpretation of the poem, then, contains within it both the Protagorean and the Socratic poles of the entire dialogue. It looks back, on the one hand, to the Sophist's techniques as a teacher; and it looks forward, on the other, to the philosophic position for which Socrates is about to argue.

Everyone, except perhaps the still reluctant Protagoras, is ready to get back to work. The best men—and Socrates is no longer joking—do not entertain themselves by relying upon the words of others. Nor are the best the happy few to whom Hippias earlier referred; they are, instead, the men who know. Since knowledge cannot be achieved by having the living attempt to extract truth from poets who are not present to tell us what they believe, the inquiry must once again take the form of dialectic. Socrates will officially resume his role as questioner and a not-quite-happy Protagoras is again the respondent.

VIII. Courage and Wisdom I (349a–351b)

There is no question about the seriousness of the final portion of the dialogue. It is dense with argument, and both Protagoras and Socrates concentrate on the business at hand. There are no further displays of temper; and while there is of course disagreement, there are also genuine signs of cooperation and good feeling.[63] Protagoras' great reluctance to make the final

---

63. See especially 351c.

admissions is soon followed by an exchange of compliments that has every appearance of being sincere (361d–e).

The issue itself is rich in implications. Protagoras now concedes that wisdom, temperance, justice, and holiness "resemble each other fairly closely" (349d3–4). The earlier arguments must have impressed him more than he was then willing to say. But on courage he does not yield: "Courage is very different from all the rest. The proof of what I say is that you can find many men who are quite unjust, unholy, intemperate, and ignorant, yet outstandingly courageous" (349d6–8).

Protagoras here asserts what everyone believes.[64] All kinds of people who are thought of as ignorant—common soldiers, athletes, and performers of various sorts of feats—are said to be courageous, while many wise and learned people are taken to be timorous and cowardly. As a spokesman of the ethic of the many, Protagoras must hold courage to be different from and independent of the other virtues; it is the strongest aspect of his thesis on the heterogeneity of the virtues.

But courage, as it is generally conceived, is also an outstanding example of a trait that is taught in the way in which Protagoras thinks of teaching. "Courage is a matter of nature and the proper nurture of the soul" (351b1–2). If that virtue is to be fostered, then, in the minds of men generally and of Protagoras in particular, it calls for the inculcation of an attitude, not for the imparting of a science; it requires training and indoctrination, rather than the development of cognitive skills.

The stakes, accordingly, are high. When Socrates sets out to refute the common view of courage and to replace it by the thesis that this virtue is tantamount to wisdom, he aims at the heart of the Protagorean enterprise. Specifically, Socrates twice sets out to demonstrate the identity of courage and wis-

---

64. This is rightly emphasized in Alexander Sesonske, "Hedonism in the *Protagoras*," *Journal of the History of Philosophy*, 1 (1963), 79.

dom. The first argument (349e–350c) does not successfully
yield its conclusion nor does it compel Protagoras' assent. The
second one (359a–360c), however, is considerably more
powerful and does exact agreement from Protagoras. The
purpose of the long interval between them (351b–359a) is
complex. Its outcome is the establishment of a premise—that
no one does evil willingly—which is required in the second
demonstration that courage is wisdom. But in the course of
getting there, Socrates argues for the truth of hedonism and
sketches out a science of human conduct. The drama of this
last part of the dialogue is almost wholly concentrated in its
arguments, and to the first of these we must now turn.

In rapid succession, Socrates secures Protagoras' assent to
two propositions:[65]

3.1. All the courageous are confident (349e).
3.2. All virtue is honorable (349e).

Then, with the aid of a few examples—daredevil divers, cav-
alrymen, and lightly armed soldiers—he has him agree that

3.3. All men who are wise are confident (350a).

But now, further observation yields agreement that

3.4. Some confident men are not wise (350b)

and, emphatically, that

3.5. No confident men who are not wise are honorable
     (350b).

Note that, so far, not a single inference has been drawn;[66]
Socrates has merely been collecting premises. Finally, how-

---

65. Again, I lean here on Vlastos' analysis (*Vlastos, 1956*, pp. xxi–xxviii)
and, in a general way, adopt his method of formulating the argument.
However, as I shall indicate, my account differs in an important way from
his.
66. Not counting the "inductions" which were cited in support of *3.3*
and *3.4*.

ever, with the aid of an uncontroversial premise that remains suppressed,

   3.6 All men who are courageous are honorable,[67]

Protagoras himself concludes that

   3.7. Some confident men are not courageous: those who are not wise (350b–c).

Socrates' procedure to this point may be summarized as follows. Confidence is a mark of courage (*3.1*), but by no means an infallible one; for *some* confident men are *not* courageous (*3.7*). To gain a proper understanding of courage, therefore, this question might be posed: what criterion will divide the class of confident men so that men who are courageous can be distinguished from those who are not? And to this an answer is suggested by the fact that those confident men who are not wise are also not courageous.

And in this spirit Socrates continues. From the claim that the "ignorantly confident show themselves *not* courageous but mad" (350c1–2), he jumps directly to the conclusion that

   3.8. All men who are wise and confident *are* courageous (350c).[68]

In short, not only does a lack of knowledge disqualify a confident man from being called courageous, but its possession qualifies him. And since all the wise are confident (*3.3*), the conclusion is reached that

   3.9. All men who are wise are courageous.[69]

---

67. As Vlastos points out; *Vlastos, 1956*, p. xxxii.

68. Literally, the text at 350c2–4 says: "And, there again, the wisest are these aforesaid and the most confident too, and as being most confident they are most courageous." (καὶ ἐκεῖ αὖ οἱ σοφώτατοι οὗτοι καὶ θαρραλεώτατοί εἰσι, θαρραλεώτατοι δὲ ὄντες ἀνδρειότατοι.)

69. Vlastos' account also has Socrates infer *3.9* from *3.3* and *3.8;* but in his view, Socrates merely asserts *3.8*, without arguing in support of it or

Clearly the argument is not valid. The fact that the ignorant are not courageous may *suggest* that the wise are, but it certainly does not entail that claim. Socrates provides premises that are adequate for showing that all the courageous are wise.[70] Wisdom is recognized to be a *necessary* condition for courage, a fact that is confirmed by the deduction of 3.7. The jump that Socrates then immediately goes on to make is to claim that wisdom is a *sufficient* condition for courage as well. The fallacy is of the commonest sort. Perhaps the most widespread error of reasoning made by ordinary people in everyday contexts is to confuse conditions that are merely necessary with sufficient ones.

Plato knew what his Socrates was about. In the first place, instead of having Protagoras agree to the conclusion, he has him make a strong statement of protest against the argument. Second, Socrates does not expend a single word in reply to Protagoras' objections, but continues right on to construct a second and much more elaborate argument in support of the same thesis that courage is wisdom.

Protagoras' own objection is both off and on the point. In his lack of clarity about the precise error in the argument, his emphatic speech says far too much. He asserts that he had not admitted that all the confident are courageous. But Socrates had never asked him to agree to this, and in the light of 3.7, he would have been foolish to do so.[71] The Sophist then goes on to complain that his original admission, that the courageous are confident, had not been shown to be in error. Yet Socrates

---

even seeking Protagoras' agreement (see *Vlastos, 1956,* p. xxxiii). If the argument is regarded in this way, however, no reason can be given as to why Socrates should have collected all the other premises; there would be no point at all to the better part of this entire passage. According to the analysis here given, Socrates does need all the propositions he has brought into the picture; indeed, he needs still more.

70. This follows readily from 3.1 and 3.5. See *Vlastos, 1956,* pp. xxiv–xxv.
71. See *ibid.,* pp. xxxiii–xxxiv.

had neither attempted such a refutation nor does his own view call for it.

If to that point Protagoras' objections are quite irrelevant to what Socrates has been saying, he then comes considerably closer to the mark: "Further, when you argue that those who have knowledge are more confident than they were before, and also than others who are ignorant, and thereupon conclude that courage and wisdom are the same thing, you might as well go on and conclude that physical strength is knowledge" (350d3-6). You are arguing,[72] Socrates (we might paraphrase), that knowledge is a *sufficient* condition of courage, on the basis of what you have just asserted (*3.8*). But all you said was that it is a necessary one. You might as well (continuing the paraphrase) derive the conclusion "wisdom is strength" (equivalent to *3.9*) from "the strong are powerful" (equivalent to *3.1*), together with "the wise are powerful" (equivalent to *3.3*), since those who know how to wrestle are more powerful than those who do not. Presumably, the intermediate steps would include equivalents of *3.7*, "some powerful men are not strong: those who are not wise," and *3.8*, "all men who are wise and powerful are strong."

Socrates does not respond, for Plato knows that there is no way to patch up this first argument. It is of a kind that is doomed to fail. Socrates has made use only of characteristics that are of the common sense, observational sort, that is, of the kind to which Protagoras is accustomed. Men are said to be courageous, confident, wise, honorable, virtuous, as if it were simply a matter of looking at them to see whether this was so. Everything is taken at face value; no *theories* about confidence, wisdom, or virtue in general are utilized or presupposed.

---

72. Not just asserting. The ἔπειτα . . . ἀποφαίνεις without the usual δέ entitles one to this translation (350d2-4).

It will be worth adding an example that is not revealed by the schematized version of the argument. When Socrates briefly supports his claim that all the wise are confident (*3.3*), he merely asserts that the knowledge of how to carry on certain types of activities makes for confidence.[73] The Greek here simply speaks of knowledge, "*epistêmê*" (350a2), so that this step should strictly have been rendered, "all those who possess knowledge about what they are doing are confident." However, when Socrates asserts that all men who are wise and confident are courageous (*3.8*), he speaks of *hoi sophôtatoi* (350c2), of the wise, so that he can come to conclude that courage is *wisdom, sophia* (350c6). Implicit in the argument, accordingly, is the view that wisdom is the sum of different knowledges and skills that are required in the performance of various activities. Wisdom, here, is just the sort of know-how which Protagoras proposes to dispense.

In sharp contrast, the thesis that courage is wisdom is far removed from observation and common sense. If it is to make any sense at all, it calls for a rethinking of the very nature of courage and of wisdom. From statements which formulate our observations about the growth of plants or the destruction of wood by fire, we do not expect to be able to deduce that the motions of Democritean atoms account for these phenomena. Democritus proposes a theory about the nature of things which is not already "contained" in our observations. In a similar way, the theory-laden conclusion as to the identity of courage and wisdom cannot be derived from statements that use only the common sense predicates to be found in Socrates' first argument. Protagoras' protest is indeed to the effect that one cannot successfully manipulate "courage," "confidence," etc., and get what Socrates wants. And in this he is correct; nor does Socrates deny it. Socrates' response, instead, is to draw Protagoras into conceptual territory that goes considerably be-

---

73. Vlastos notes this and points out the inadequacy of the "induction." See *Vlastos, 1956*, pp. xxxvi–xxxviii.

neath the level of observation, into a theory about all of human motivation and about the nature of goodness in general.

IX. THE INVOLUNTARINESS OF EVIL (351b–358d)

The explicit point of this section of the dialogue is to establish the proposition that no one willingly seeks evil,[74] a thesis Socrates then employs to demonstrate once again that courage is wisdom. But from the point of view of sheer efficiency, this portion of the dialogue is superfluous. Protagoras agrees at the outset that "knowledge is an honorable[75] thing quite capable of ruling a man, and if he can distinguish good from evil, nothing will force him to act otherwise than as knowledge dictates, since wisdom (*phronêsis*) is all the reinforcement he needs" (352c2–7). If the power of knowledge is as great as this, it also follows that men cannot willingly do evil.[76] Nevertheless, Socrates proceeds with his argument, for the many are held to believe that "it is not the knowledge (*epistêmê*) that a man possesses which governs him, but something else—now passion, now pleasure, now pain, sometimes love, and frequently fear" (352b5–c2). What follows, we are frequently reminded, is addressed to the many, with Protagoras responding in their behalf. And, to make utterly sure that we do not forget, Socrates later begins a summary of the argument by recalling that "we two agreed that there was nothing more powerful than knowledge, but that wherever it is found it always has the mastery over pleasure and everything else" (357c1–4).

For Protagoras, the question about the power of knowledge

---

74. A discussion of the precise formulation of Socrates' thesis will have to await Sec. X.

75. καλόν. Guthrie sayes "fine."

76. See Sec. X for an account of this implication.

is a dilemma. As a teacher of virtue, his career would seem to be justified only if knowledge makes a genuine difference to the lives of his pupils: "I above all men should think it shame to speak of wisdom and knowledge (*sophia* and *epistêmê*) as anything but the most powerful elements in human life" (352d1–3). And yet, this is a superficial response, dictated more by Protagoras' vanity as a professional and the imposing ring of the words *sophia* and *epistêmê*. We know that there is another side to Protagoras as well. He has no doctrine of virtue of his own, but claims merely to make explicit the views that are embedded in the customs and practices of the societies to which his students belong. His teaching, then, does not consist of the imparting of knowledge of what men are really like and of what true virtue is. The multitude, moreover, was early on shown to hold that virtue is "taught" in the training that is given to children by all those who participate in the initiation of the young into the society into which they are born. Protagoras had explicitly associated himself with these teachers of the youth of Greece. But if such is the teacher's task, he provides nurture,[77] rather than knowledge; he inculcates attitudes, and does not set forth what is true. A more deliberate Protagoras, one whose vanity was not aroused by the presence of an audience composed of competitors, admirers, and pupils—actual and potential—would not so quickly have been drawn out of the realm of common sense into the philosophic doctrine which maintains that no one willingly does evil. Instead, he would have put up a struggle against Socrates' dialectic.

With great skill, Plato reveals to us at one and the same time two sides of the great Sophist: the professional teacher with his public stance and the philosophic unphilosopher who, in his role as defender of the multitude, is progressively drawn

---

77. "Courage," Protagoras had said, "is a matter of nature and the proper nurture ($\varepsilon\dot{v}\tau\rho o\phi\acute{\iota}\alpha s$) of the soul" (351b1–2).

into philosophy by the power of dialectic. The argument of this section, then, supports a thesis which Protagoras *says* he holds, although this is in fact not the case. It thus proceeds to foist upon the Sophist—not without resistance!—a position he was willing to grant at the outset.

The method by which Socrates demonstrates the involuntariness of evil has complexities of its own.[78] He first sets out to show that all pleasures are good and that all goods are pleasure (*4.1–4.9*) and then offers two arguments in refutation of the popular view that men do evil because they are overcome by pleasure (*5.1–5.5* and *6.1–6.5*). The next argument supports the claim that making erroneous choices depends upon ignorance (*7.1–7.8*), a proposition that is then used to establish, finally, that no one does evil willingly (*8.1–8.5*). Each of these arguments will be taken up in turn.

Socrates begins by asking Protagoras whether he is prepared to agree that all pleasures are good and all pains are evil (*4.91*). But Protagoras refuses and declares that he shares the view of the many that some pleasures are evil and some pains good (351d). What Socrates has asserted is merely the claim that pleasure, taken in itself, is *a* good and pain, taken in itself, is *an* evil, a doctrine "to which the overwhelming majority of philosophical moralists, ancient and modern, would subscribe."[79] But, like the multitude, Protagoras disagrees with this proposition, so that Socrates is not free to utilize it as a premise in his argument. Very sensibly, Protagoras suggests that the matter be investigated.

At this point the discussion takes a sharp turn. Let us examine, Protagoras proposes, whether "pleasant and good are

---

78. For what follows I am greatly indebted to Gregory Vlastos, "Socrates on Acrasia," *Phoenix*, 23 (1969), henceforth to be referred to as *Vlastos, 1969*. Yet once again, the fact that I place Socrates' arguments into the context of the dialogue as a whole leads me to somewhat different conclusions on a number of issues.

79. *Vlastos, 1969*, p. 76.

found to be the same" (351e5–6); he thus goes much further than Socrates had.[80] Only now—and by Protagoras—is hedonism brought into the picture. To inquire as to whether "pleasure and good are found to be the same" does not merely raise the question as to whether all pleasures are good, but also whether all goods are pleasures (4.92), whether pleasure, that is, is the *only* good and pain the *sole* evil.

Socrates now goes on to establish the proposition that constitutes the hedonist's view, but a puzzle is created thereby. He himself had not put hedonism forward as his own view, while the many and Protagoras were not even willing to assent to the weaker claim that all pleasures are good. Socrates, then, is about to persuade Protagoras of a thesis—that no one does evil willingly—which Protagoras professes to hold (but really does not) by means of a premise—that pleasure is the only good—which he professes *not* to maintain. An odd way to convince an opponent!

Yet again, if we look beneath what Protagoras professes explicitly, the essential instability of his view becomes manifest. Once more we see Protagoras attempting to take a stand at a place that does not exist: between popular morality, just as it is professed by the common man, and a philosophic ethics that calls for a doctrine about the nature of man and the good. Protagoras, in his role as teacher without a doctrine of his own, sides with the many who hold that there are bad pleasures.[81] But as the teacher of virtue who is superior to parents and poets, it is Protagoras' method to probe beneath the level of what men say and to formulate the view that is actually em-

---

80. The text says τὸ αὐτὸ φαίνηται ἡδύ τε καὶ ἀγαθόν. See *Vlastos, 1969*, pp. 76–78, which is particularly helpful on this.

81. Gerasimos Santas is surely not correct in thinking that hedonism is a belief of the many—certainly not in the sense that the man in the street (whether of Athens or of New York) would reply in the negative to either of the following questions: Are there any pleasures that are bad? Are there any goods that are not pleasant? See Gerasimos Santas, "Plato's *Protagoras* and Explanations of Weakness," *The Philosophical Review*, 75 (1966), 8, n. 7; henceforth cited as *Santas, 1966*.

bedded in what they *do*. With malice aforethought, Socrates assists Protagoras in that enterprise, but in doing so demonstrates to him as well that he is forced to assume a philosophic position. Specifically, a closer look at the position implicit in the practice of men reveals them to be hedonists in spite of what they say, a revelation which, by his own conception of his role, forces Protagoras to embrace hedonism himself. The premise that is needed to persuade Protagoras of the truth of what he says he holds (but in fact needs to be forced to maintain)—that no one willingly does evil—is a proposition that Protagoras (though he says he does not hold it) is in fact committed to—that pleasure is the only good.[82]

In his argument, Socrates proposes to show that hedonism is implicit in the common view. He interrogates the many in exactly the fashion called for by Protagoras' own program. The multitude believes that there are bad pleasures; hence it is possible that

4.1. M does *A* which is pleasant, but evil (353c).

However, the many would surely not deny that pleasure itself is good; hence

4.2. A is not evil *because* it is pleasant (353d),

but rather, the many could not think of a reason other than that

4.3. A is evil because it causes pain (353d–e).

In a perfectly analogous way, Socrates then turns to pain:

4.4. M does *B* which is painful, but good (354a).
4.5. B is not good *because* it is painful (354b).
4.6. B is good because it causes pleasure (354b).

---

82. There may be a modicum of awareness of this commitment in Protagoras' switch to hedonism from Socrates' original and weaker claim. I do not see that Protagoras is rattled, as Vlastos maintains (*Vlastos, 1969*, p. 77, n. 24), when, at 351e7, he identifies good and pleasure. He does so in a very calm and deliberate "let us examine together" passage.

Socrates' next step is implied by *4.2* and *4.5*:

4.7. All pleasures are good and all pains evil (354c–e);

while *4.3* and *4.6* yields him

4.8. There is no other standard of good and evil besides pleasure and pain (354c–e).

And this is tantamount to the two propositions which together make up the hedonist position:

4.91. All pleasures are good and all pains are evil.
4.92. All goods are pleasure and all evils are pain.

The many are asked here to reflect on the criteria they actually use in day-to-day judgments and have it revealed to them, under Socrates' pressure, that their profession that some pleasures are bad is merely that and plays no role in their behavior. For someone who attaches no ultimate significance to how the many actually make judgments of value, this is no proof of ethical hedonism. For Protagoras, however, it is the only admissible kind of demonstration, precisely because it makes explicit the position that underlies the practice of the multitude.[83]

Before continuing, Socrates offers the many an opportunity to retract and warns them that the argument to follow depends on the conclusion just reached. But they cannot come up with any other standard of goodness: Protagoras makes no move in their behalf. Socrates is thus free to go on and show that a common account of evildoing is wrong: no one does evil simply because he is overcome by pleasure.[84] Specifically, Socrates produces two arguments that take the form of a

---

83. See J. P. Sullivan, "The Hedonism in Plato's *Protagoras*," *Phronesis*, 6 (1961), 22–24.

84. Santas rightly points out that henceforth Socrates argues only against the explanation of evildoing that involves pleasure. Nothing is said about the power of love or fear. On the relation of Socrates' argument to arguments that might be directed against accounts of evildoing which depend upon love or fear, see *Santas, 1966,* especially Sec. III.

reductio ad absurdum of a commonly held view assumed to be true at the outset.[85]

5.1. M chooses *A* over *B*, knowing that *B* is better than *A*, because *M* is overcome by the pleasures of *A* (355a–b).

But then, using *4.91*, we get

5.2. M chooses *A* over *B*, knowing that *B* is better than *A*, because *M* is overcome by the goods of *A* (355c).

Now, since *M* is subject to censure, *A* must contain fewer goods than *B*, so that

5.3. M chooses *A* over *B*, knowing that *B* is better than *A*, because *M* is overcome by the goods of *A*, where *A* contains fewer goods than *B* (355d).

But, and this premise remains tacit,[86]

5.4. M always chooses what he takes to be the greater aggregate of goods over the lesser,

from which it follows that

5.5. The original assumption, *5.1*, is absurd, since it entails *5.3*, which in turn is incompatible with *5.4*.

This intitial argument calls for two comments. In the first place, Socrates reaches his conclusion without utilizing the premise of hedonism. The substitution in *5.1* that yields *5.2* calls only for the assumption that pleasure is *a* good, but not that it is the only good. Protagoras has been shown to be a hedonist in spite of himself, but Socrates has not utilized that position. Nor does he require it to establish the premise he needs in order to show the sameness of wisdom and courage.

---

85. I follow Vlastos in holding that Socrates makes two arguments here. See *Vlastos, 1969*, pp. 85–87.

86. See *Vlastos, 1969*, pp. 81–85, where the role of this step is discussed. Also see my comments immediately below.

In the subsequent stages that lead to this conclusion, we shall see that the hedonist thesis can always be detached without harm to the argument; at this point Socrates simply offers an argument in which that assumption plays no role at all.

Second, there is the tacit premise, *5.4*, without which the conclusion could not be reached. It asserts, in effect, that men always seek their own welfare or the means thereto, a tenet latter-day textbooks call psychological egotism. That men are in a more or less enlightened way self-interested is either made explicit or assumed in all Platonic dialogues in which the matter is relevant.[87] Plato never finds himself asking seriously whether men do indeed desire their own welfare; he is concerned, instead, with the *nature* of that welfare.[88] Not only does Plato hold the tacit premise to be true, but he would have no reason to suppose that any of his readers would deny it, any more than Aristotle would think that there could be a difference between what is good for a man to do and what man's good is. Indeed, it may well be that the premise remains tacit, not because Plato thought it unnecessary to state it, but because it never occurred to him at all to make it explicit.

Since Protagoras was forced to embrace the hedonist assumption, the dialogue continues with Socrates once again reducing a common explanation of evildoing to absurdity—this time by using the thesis that pleasure is the only good.

---

87. This point is argued in Gerasimos Santas, "The Socratic Paradoxes," *The Philosophical Review,* 73 (1964), 150–57; in *Santas, 1966,* especially p. 22; and in *Vlastos, 1969,* pp. 83ff. Also see Sullivan, "The Hedonism in Plato's *Protagoras,*" pp. 19–21.

88. In short, Plato qualifies as an ethical egotist as well. The use of "rightly" (ὀρθῶς) and "usefully" or "advantageously" (ὠφελίμως) as if they came to the same thing (332a6–7; see pp. 82, 87–88, above) suggests that Socrates and Protagoras in our dialogue also hold that view. If one holds that men ought to seek their own welfare, one does not *need* to believe that men in fact always do so; most ethical egotists, however, think of themselves as preaching that men should be more enlightened, in some specific way, in going after what they seek in the first place.

6.1. M chooses A over B, knowing that B is better than A, because M is overcome by the pleasures of A (355e–356a).

Substitution in *6.1*, now by means of *4.92*, yields

6.2. M chooses A over B, knowing that B is more pleasant than A, because M is overcome by the pleasures of A, where A contains fewer pleasures than B (355e–356a).[89]

Then, assuming pleasure to be the *only* good (that is, taking both *4.91* and *4.92*), it follows that

6.3. Pleasures can differ from each other only in magnitude (356a–b).

For his next step, Socrates explicitly formulates the assumption of psychological hedonism:

6.4. M will always choose (what he takes to be) the greater magnitude of pleasure over the lesser (356b–c).

And since, as in the previous argument, *6.1* entails *6.2*, which in turn is incompatible with *6.4*, Socrates concludes that

6.5. The original assumption, *6.1*, is absurd (356c).

Not only does this argument require the assumption that pleasure is the only good (in the move to *6.2*), but it also supposes that "in weighing pleasures against pleasures, one *must* always choose the greater and the more" (356b3–4). No fuss whatever is made over the introduction here of psychological hedonism (*6.4*), for it follows readily from what has gone before. If we assume ethical hedonism to be established and we suppose, further, that men always seek their own welfare, it

---

89. For simplicity's sake, the references to pain are left out here and below, and it is assumed, with Socrates, that pleasure and pain can be considered to belong to a single continuum.

follows that men will always desire the greater pleasure, for their welfare must reside in pleasure—the only good there is.[90]

Socrates has now eliminated the popular account of evildoing and next sets out to give a more adequate explanation of his own. His ultimate aim is to establish that men do evil out of ignorance. But before he is ready to support this claim, he first argues that ignorance is responsible for the erroneous choices men make in life. Yet in spite of the merely intermediary role of this sequence of steps, the passage we are about to discuss is in some ways the high point of the dialogue. Here, more than elsewhere, is Protagoras drawn into Socrates' philosophic territory; here it is made manifest to him what sort of enterprise teaching virtue really is. While a schematic representation of the argument will once again be helpful, it will not do justice to its importance.

Using the examples of thickness, number, and loudness, Socrates and Protagoras agree that

> *7.1.* Magnitudes that are in fact equal appear to be greater when observed from near than from far (356c–d).

Given this fact, we are readily led to see that

> *7.2.* In judging magnitudes we can be led into error by this power of appearance (356d)

and to prescribe a method for overcoming the power of appearance:

> *7.3.* Judging magnitudes correctly depends on an art[91] of measurement (356d–e).

---

90. In the light of these implications, the fact that Socrates so casually and without objection introduces psychological hedonism into the argument corroborates the claim that the truth of ethical egotism was taken for granted by all participants in the dialogue.

91. First τέχνη (at 356d4), then τέχνη καὶ ἐπιστήμη at (357b4).

Then, if we make explicit what an art of measurement is, we may say that

> 7.4. Such an art of measurement is knowledge (357a).

Now, given that pleasure is the only good (*4.91* and *4.92*) and that pleasures can differ from each other only in magnitude,

> 7.5. Making correct choices in life[92] depends upon judging correctly magnitudes of pleasures and pains (357a–b).

Thus, given *7.3*, we may say that

> 7.6. Judging magnitudes of pleasure and pain correctly depends on an art of measurement of pleasures and pains (357a–b).

Finally, since *7.4* and since ignorance is the opposite of knowledge and error the opposite of correctness, it follows that

> 7.7. Making erroneous choices in life depends upon lack of knowledge, or ignorance (357d–e).

Socrates could have reached his conclusion more expeditiously. Because men choose what will give them the greatest aggregate of pleasure, making correct choices depends upon knowing what is most pleasurable, while failing to do so is a consequence of ignorance or false opinion regarding pleasures and pains. Instead, be begins by taking up magnitudes in general. Ordinary observation, Socrates maintains, is deceptive; we mistake the sizes of things, their thickness, their number, and the real strength of different sounds. But we do not have to make errors in judging such magnitudes. Protagoras and everyone else in the audience know that there are sciences—arithmetic, geometry, music—which consist of a coherent

---

92. Choices that will secure our "welfare" ($\sigma\omega\tau\eta\rho\iota\alpha$) (357a6).

body of rational principles about such magnitudes and of established procedures for handling them. These sciences are capable of counteracting the misleading character of so much of casual observation and of conducting us to conclusions that are in accord with the true nature of the magnitudes in question. If anything is knowledge and is recognized as such, it is this domain of mathematics. And now Socrates reveals that if men are to secure their own welfare in life, they must come into possession of a science of exactly the same sort. Knowledge of the magnitudes of pleasures and pains is both a necessary and a sufficient condition for the achievement of just the kind of life to which the Sophists profess to assist their pupils.

Hippias' teaching—and both Hippias and Prodicus are now explicitly brought back into the conversation[93]—includes the established sciences in its curriculum. But their purpose is to contribute to the production of a cultured gentleman. No ingredient in Hippias' polymathy is actually a science of conduct; no part of the education he provides consists of a methodology for the making of choices that will tend to increase the welfare of the student. Protagoras rejects this omnifarious approach to education; remember his significant glance in Hippias' direction at 318e. Yet what he substitutes in his more single-minded pursuit of *aretê* is neither a system of truths nor a method by means of which such truths may be obtained, but rather a miscellany of attitudes, skills, and knacks that are not at all knowledge in the way our knowledge of mathematics is.

The many had believed that wrong choices typically were made because the agent was overcome by pleasure. But why, then, should they spend good money on an education from the Sophists, if it is really true that "ignorance [is] the fault which Protagoras, Prodicus, and Hippias profess to cure" (357e2–4)? Yet now, when it turns out that the multitude is wrong in its account of bad choices, and ignorance *is* shown to be its cause,

---

93. At 357e and 358a, for the first time since the session on Simonides' poem.

it becomes clear that what the Sophists *do* is not at all what they profess. From raw material gathered out of the beliefs that are shared, in obvious and in veiled ways, by both the many and Protagoras, Socrates has fashioned an exhibit of what is possible: a science of conduct—unquestionably knowledge—which, when acquired by the student, will lead him to the better life Protagoras promises. By showing how the *philosophic* development of his own presuppositions can lead to a solution of the very problem he seeks to solve, Socrates has most effectively subjected to criticism the unphilosophic way of Protagoras.[94]

Socrates is now prepared to return to the business immediately at hand. If erroneous judgments in life depend upon ignorance, no one willingly does evil. It had earlier been agreed (*4.91*) that

> *8.1* All pleasures are good and all pains evil (358a).

And since the pursuit of what is good is honorable,[95]

> *8.2.* All actions that aim at living pleasantly and painlessly are honorable and good (358b).

But because men choose what they take to yield the greater pleasure (*6.4*) and because ignorance accounts for erroneous choices (*7.7*),

> *8.3.* No one who knows that action A is more pleasant than action B willingly chooses B (358b–c),

which, using *8.1* and taking it to hold in the comparative, yields

---

94. Socrates has not given a Platonic account of knowledge. Rather, he has created a kind of model of the scientific enterprise out of the materials that are accepted as knowledge by the members of his audience. Socrates is drawing Protagoras into philosophy by exhibiting to him the superior characteristics of a hedonistic calculus; he is not thereby putting forth what he takes to be the true philosophy.

95. See *3.2*, p. 104, above.

> *8.4.* No one who knows that action *A* is better than action *B* willingly chooses *B* (358c)

and

> *8.5.* Whoever does choose action *B* (the worse) does so not willingly, but out of ignorance (358c),

where ignorance is understood to mean "having a false opinion and being mistaken on matters of great moment" (356c4–5).

Foreshadowing a later Platonic analysis of the psyche, Socrates now calls wisdom "being one's own master" (358c3) and identifies "giving in to oneself" (358c2) with ignorance. Men do not do evil because they are overcome by pleasure, but because they are ignorant. Socrates has replaced the popular explanation by a philosophic one and has established the premise he needs to demonstrate that courage is wisdom.[96]

X. Courage and Wisdom II (358d–360a)

The last argument of the dialogue once again attacks Protagoras' thesis of the heterogeneity of the virtues at their strongest point and seeks to show that even courage is wisdom. Plato depicts a Protagoras who is aware of the damage that is being done to his position, for as the argument progresses, the Sophist becomes more and more reluctant to give his assent. The argument is long and complex; comments are best postponed until after it has been stated.

The initial premise is a version of the conclusion that was just reached (*8.5*), one which will call for subsequent discussion.[97]

---

96. Some further comments on this argument will be found in the next section.

97. For simplicity's sake, I have substituted throughout the entire argument "chooses" for phrases such as "willingly goes after" (ἰέναι ἐπί τι or λαμβάνειν τι). This does justice to the element of voluntariness, while still remaining neutral regarding the success or failure of any *action*.

9.01. No one chooses to do what he knows or thinks to be evil (358c–d).

Then, agreeing that

9.02. Fear is the expectation of evil (358d),

it follows, in general, that

9.03. No one chooses to do what he fears (358e)

and, more specifically, that

9.04. Neither cowards nor the courageous choose to do what is fearful, but rather what is not fearful (359c–d).

But, since courage and cowardice are opposites,

9.05. Cowards and the courageous choose to do opposite things (359c, e).

Now, it is not a matter of controversy that

9.06. The courageous choose to do what is honorable (359e)

and that

9.07. The courageous choose to do what is good (359e);[98]

nor, given *9.05,* that

9.08. Cowards do not choose to do what is honorable and good (360a).

Earlier it was shown that *4.91* and *4.92.;* hence

9.09 Whatever is honorable and good is pleasant (360a).

The next two premises remain tacit, but they follow readily from *9.08* and *9.09*:

---

98. See *3.1–3.6*, pp. 104–105, above.

9.10. Cowards do not choose to do what is honorable, good, and pleasant;

9.11. Cowards choose to do what is disgraceful, evil, and painful.

This, given a version of *9.01* (e.g., "if anyone chooses to do evil, he does not know that it is evil"), yields

9.12. Cowards do not choose to do what is disgraceful, evil, and painful, knowing that it is such (360a).

From *9.06, 9.07,* and *9.09,* we get

9.13. The courageous choose to do what is honorable, good, and pleasant (360a).

And since courage is a virtue, the next three premises may be asserted:

9.14. The boldness (and fear) of the courageous is not disgraceful (360b);

9.15. The boldness (and fear) of the courageous is honorable (360b);

9.16. The boldness (and fear) of the courageous is good (360b).

From *9.15* and *9.05,* it follows that

9.17. The fear of cowards (and the boldness of the mad) is disgraceful (360b).

But since *9.12,* we may also say that

9.18. The cause of the cowards' disgraceful fear (and the mads' boldness) is ignorance (360b).

However, it was earlier agreed that any act of a certain kind is a function of a faculty or agency of that kind (*2.08*),[99] so that

---

99. See p. 80, above.

> *9.19.* The cause of cowards being cowardly is cowardice (360c),

which, together with *9.18,* yields

> *9.20.* Cowardice is ignorance of what is and is not fearful (360c).

From this crucial step and the next two uncontroversial premises,

> *9.21.* Courage is the opposite of cowardice (360c–d)

and

> *9.22.* Wisdom of what is and is not fearful is the opposite of the ignorance of these (360d),

Socrates reaches his final conclusion that

> *9.23.* Courage is wisdom of what is and is not fearful (360d).

As the argument nears its conclusion, Protagoras becomes more and more unhappy. After the assertion of *9.12,* he qualifies his assent by noting that if this step were not agreed to we should "confound our former conclusions" (360a6). He "feels forced to admit" *9.13* (360a8); at *9.20* he merely nods (360c7). While at *9.22* "he could still nod assent" (360d3) and when *9.20* is reasserted, Protagoras agrees "with great reluctance" (360d3–4), the final conclusion (*9.23*) is too much for him: "he could no longer bring himself to assent, but was silent" (360d6).

These passages show more than that Protagoras is dismayed by the *conclusion* of the argument—as well he might be, for it contradicts his own view of the nature of the virtues. They indicate, as well, that Protagoras feels forced to accept it by Socrates' dialectic. And yet why should he permit himself to be compelled by the argument? Its very first premise had been demonstrated by means of an argument with which Protag-

oras was not himself associated.[100] The many had maintained
that men do evil because they are overcome by pleasure, but
Protagoras had explicitly rejected this. Why, then, it is well
worth asking again, did Protagoras not go beyond reluctance;
why did he not object more fundamentally to Socrates' procedure? "I am perfectly willing," he might have said, "to continue the inquiry and to see what follows from the views of the
multitude, as long as you remember that my own beliefs are
in no way affected by the argument you are making." Yet
Protagoras was right to be discouraged; for such a protest
sounds hollow indeed. Protagoras *is* affected by the culminat-
ing argument of the *Protagoras,* and I now wish to take up
three separate reasons why this is so.

(*1*) We must recall that before the many were ever brought
into the picture, Protagoras agreed "that knowledge is a fine
thing quite capable of ruling a man, and that if he can distinguish good from evil, nothing will force him to act otherwise[101] than as knowledge dictates, since wisdom is all the
reinforcement he needs" (352c3–7). An examination of what
this agreement comes to will show that it is sufficient to yield
Socrates' first premise (*9.01*).[102]

We are *not* concerned with action. The power of knowledge
is not praised, here or elsewhere in the dialogue, as conquer-
ing *all*. Someone may know of two alternatives, *A* and *B,* and
knowing that *A* is better, may choose to do *A,* but be prevented from carrying out *A* by external circumstances or by
lack of power. He can (in *this* sense) be forced to act otherwise, which does not mean that he can be forced to *choose*
otherwise. The statement denies that, in the face of knowledge

---

100. The same is true of such other steps as *9.09,* which depend upon
the hedonist thesis.

101. μὴ ἂν κρατηθῆναι ὑπὸ μηδενός, ὥστε ἀλλ᾽ ἄττα πράττειν (352c5–6).
This is emphatic language indeed.

102. It will also provide an opportunity to comment further on that
premise itself.

of what is right, some other motive or impulse—passion, pleasure, pain, love[103]—can force a man to choose to do *B*.

Let us consider a man who does not know that *A* is better than *B*. In such a case, three quite different possibilities are open: (*i*) he may have no opinion about the relative merits of *A* and *B*; (*ii*) he may believe *B* to be better than *A*, although *A* is in fact better than *B*; or (*iii*) he may believe *A* to be better than *B*, where *A* *is* better than *B*, but not *know* this to be the case.

(*i*) A man may lack an opinion about the relative merits of *A* and *B*, simply because he does not think about the alternatives at all, and act impulsively or unconsciously. But then he would not be "seeking to meet" or be "going after" some result or other in a way that would justify our thinking of him as acting willingly, voluntarily, intentionally, or from choice. In that case we are not even discussing the issue with which Socrates is concerned.[104] But if a man *does* think, yet without thinking that either *A* or *B* is the better of the alternatives, what could he be thinking about? That *A* is more pleasant, that it is a means to *C* which constitutes the avoidance of a danger, and so on. Here Socrates' psychological egotism comes into play: when a man chooses, he does so because he takes what he chooses to contribute to his welfare,[105] so that if he chose one alternative as more pleasant or because it was the means to the avoidance of a danger or whatever, he would be choosing it *as* the greater contribution to the aggregate of goods he will have in life—that is, *as* goods or as means thereto.

---

103. These are the ones mentioned at 352b.

104. This case, by way of digression, suggests a reply in behalf of the many, regarding their theory that an evildoer is overcome by pleasure. Perhaps the prospect of immediate pleasure prevents a man from thinking altogether, so as to induce him to act without choosing at all. While this is not the view actually attributed to the many, it gives their position some semblance of correctness.

105. Protagoras attracts his students on the basis of the truth of this. They come to him because they want to do what is good for them and to learn from him how to identify goods and how to secure them.

But now, a man might be *wrong* in his belief and (*ii*) think wrongly that *B* is better than *A*. He will then choose to do what he wrongly believes to be better precisely because he has that erroneous belief. He will "go after" evil because he lacked the power of knowledge.

The last case (*iii*) considers someone who is in possession of true opinion about the relative merit of alternatives, but not of knowledge. The first thing that must be said about this instance is that Socrates does not consider it. Socrates' entire account of men's judgments about magnitudes is given solely in terms of knowledge and *false* belief. When Socrates contrasts the power of appearance with the power of knowledge,[106] he speaks of a power that deceives and leads to *erroneous* opinions about magnitudes—as over and against the (correct) knowledge of the art of measurement. Knowledge is not pitted against *mere* opinion, but against *false* opinion, a fact that is made fully explicit when ignorance, the opposite of knowledge, is defined as "having a false opinion and being mistaken on matters of great moment" (358c4–5).[107]

If, now, we nevertheless take up the case of true opinion, we can agree with Vlastos[108] that, compared with the surefootedness of knowledge, this state is indeed unstable and a man might not hold on to his correct belief for very long. As a consequence of this, true belief may well not be sufficient for *doing* the right thing, for a man may change his mind before he actually carries out his (accidental, lucky) correct choice. (So, if we are going to *act* to secure our welfare, to have the *knowledge* provided by the art of measurement helps.) But the issue is not acting, but choosing. Given that men always seek what is best for them, true opinion, however briefly held,

---

106. See 356d–357a.

107. τὸ ψευδῆ ἔχειν δόξαν καὶ ἐψεῦσθαι περὶ τῶν πραγμάτων τῶν πολλοῦ ἀξίων.

108. *Vlastos, 1969,* pp. 72–73.

if it leads to a choice at all, is sufficient to assure a correct choice.

Socrates and Protagoras thus agree that the power of knowledge is great, but they are, on the same grounds, in agreement that ignorance is equally powerful. Knowledge guarantees that the right choice will be made, while ignorance —believing falsely that a proposed action is right—guarantees that the choice will be wrong. On no occasion can a man choose to do what he thinks to be wrong. The agreement on the power of knowledge entails the first and crucial premise in Socrates' last argument on courage (*9.01*), that no one chooses what he knows or thinks to be evil.[109]

Once the issue of this key premise is resolved, the rest of the argument, in all its length, can go through without the assumption of hedonism. It would seem that the contrary is the case. Only if pleasure were thought to be the only good could *9.09* be maintained; pleasure (or pain) is brought in at each of the next four steps (*9.10–9.13*), although the first two of these remain unexpressed. But note that *9.09* is only used to enable Socrates to add the predicate "pleasant" or "painful" to "honorable" and "good" or "disgraceful" and "evil" in the four steps mentioned. The argument would in no way be impaired by their omission, especially since in all the subsequent steps Socrates once again drops all reference to pleasure or pain. In short, if one takes Protagoras to agree that knowledge is all-powerful in the soul, the rest of the argument can compel his

---

109. At 358b–c, Socrates thrice states that the *belief* that a course of action is evil sufficient to prevent a man from pursuing it, whereas earlier (352c, etc.) he had spoken only of knowledge. Because of the sharp contrast Socrates makes between the power of appearance and that of knowledge, Vlastos suggests that Socrates, without actually saying so, means "that we cannot act contrary to what we believe *when we do have knowledge*" (*Vlastos, 1969*, p. 73; italics in original). But we have seen that the differentiation between appearance and knowledge is not relevant to the question of true belief and that no problem is raised by the version of the premise as it appears here.

assent to the claim that courage is wisdom without the assumption of hedonism.

(2) Suppose, however, that we took Protagoras' willingness to accord so great a power to knowledge to be merely a product of his professional role, supported by a healthy dose of vanity. Yet even if we thought that Protagoras did not really mean to concede that knowledge rules a man, the proposition that no one does evil willingly can be derived without resort to hedonism. In the final argument (8.1–8.5) of the sequence that leads to this conclusion, the proposition that formulates the principle of psychological egotism (8.4) is in effect deduced from a formulation of psychological hedonism (6.4) that had earlier been asserted.[110] But whatever may be the case about the doctrine that all men always choose what they take to be the greatest aggregate of *pleasure,* it has already been pointed out that both Socrates and Protagoras are committed to the thesis that men always aim to secure their own welfare. And, with appropriate qualifications regarding men's knowledge of what is good for them, this proposition suffices for the demonstration of the crucial premise in the concluding argument for the equivalence of courage and wisdom (8.5 or 9.01).

The two considerations just put forward show not only why Protagoras should, however unhappily, feel constrained to yield to Socrates' final argument, but they reveal as well that Socrates was capable of demonstrating his claim regarding the relation of wisdom and courage without utilizing the controversial principle of hedonism. That Socrates does not ultimately depend upon hedonism to support so characteristically Socratic a doctrine as that courage is wisdom constitutes further, if indirect, proof that the character Plato calls "Socrates" in this particular dialogue did not hold the hedonist position.[111]

---

110. At 356b–c. See p. 117, above.

111. Vlastos, in addition, shows that Socrates can reach the conclusion that no one does evil willingly by means of the proposition that pleasure

(3) Finally, it must be recalled that in spite of his disavowal, Protagoras *is* committed to hedonism. Undoubtedly his reluctance to yield to Socrates' dialectic is in part based upon the fact that hedonism is *not* needed to secure his assent to the last set of fatal steps. Nevertheless, Protagoras' resistance is also grounded in his awareness that his entire enterprise requires him to hold some form of hedonism. The argument against the multitude goes along until the state of being overcome by pleasure is replaced by ignorance as an explanation for evildoing. At that moment (358a), Socrates once again draws in his immediate audience and addresses Prodicus, Hippias, and Protagoras by name. Yet what he then says has no direct connection with what has just transpired. "You agree then . . . that the pleasant is good and the painful bad" (358a5–6): Protagoras is asked to assent to the very sentence to which he had earlier taken exception (351d), and he, together with the other Sophists present, agrees without a murmur.[112] While the full assumption of hedonism is not brought in until a moment later,[113] Protagoras' lack of protest at this point must be taken as an expression of his—at least partial—awareness that he is committed to the doctrine. Protagoras is right to be unhappy about the course of the debate; he has no choice but to accept the conclusion Socrates seeks to establish.

XI. Conclusion (360e–362a)

Young Hippocrates had started it all, for he had wanted to become a pupil of Protagoras. At the outset of the discussion with Protagoras, Socrates had been dubious that virtue could be taught, whereas the Sophist confidently explained how

---

is *a* good and without assuming that pleasure is the *only* good. See *Vlastos, 1969*, pp. 86–87.

112. This is the agreement to *8.1;* see p. 121, above.

113. It is implied by *8.3;* see *ibid.*

everyone teaches virtue. Now, in Socrates' words, the subject is in "utter confusion" (361c2–3), for the two protagonists appear to have reversed their positions. Socrates has been intent on showing that the different virtues are all "a single whole, knowledge" (361b1–2), which would make them most eminently teachable, while Protagoras has been strenuously resisting this identification which, if he were thought successful, would make virtue "least likely to be teachable" (361c1–2).

Socrates is anxious to clear up the confusion by turning next to examine the nature of virtue directly and by then coming back to the question of its teachability. He concludes by assuring Protagoras that it is with him that he "would most gladly share the inquiry" (361d6). Protagoras returns the compliment by expressing his admiration for Socrates and by predicting a great future for him as a philosopher. Right now, however, "it is time to turn to other things" (361e6). Socrates goes off to keep an appointment, if belatedly, and the dialogue comes to an end.

But there is no reversal, no confusion; yet neither are there conclusions, nor has anything been established. There is no reversal, because Protagoras and Socrates conceive of virtue and of teaching in sharply divergent ways. What the Sophist maintains is teachable is the set of criteria of what it means to be successful in action, as these standards are imbedded in common practice. Teaching, for him, is the inculcation of skills and attitudes that will lead to the student's smooth functioning in his particular society. Socrates never denies that *this* virtue is teachable in *that* sense of teaching. It would be blindness not to see that Protagoras makes sound observations in his great speech. All societies more or less successfully perpetuate their customs and conventions by means of the effect that parents, nurses, teachers, laws, and institutions have upon children and citizens.

Socrates is most skeptical, however, about the claim that what Protagoras calls virtue is teachable in the way in which geometry or harmony are taught. For in this kind of teaching —and for Socrates it is the only kind—a body of truths that are grounded in demonstrations and measurements appropriate to the subject matter come to be seen, to be comprehended, by the pupil. And as *Socrates* conceives of virtue, it must be in *his* sense teachable. Whatever virtue is—and the inquiry into that subject has yet to take place—it must be rooted in the nature of man as such and of the good and not merely in the happenstance practices of a particular time and place, just as truths about the relations holding among the parts of a triangle are independent of the diagram that is drawn to demonstrate them. Socrates has never changed his position, although that of Protagoras was put under severe pressure.

And there is no confusion. The dialogue exhibits the way of Socrates and the way of Protagoras and shows them in conflict with each other. Protagoras' method and manner are in harmony with the relationship he has to his audience and clientele. We see him in his ambiguous role as both teacher and entertainer: eloquent and persuasive in his speeches, clever in his lessons, combative in dialogue. Protagoras has the answers; Socrates has none: he is all inquirer. But while Protagoras is naive and fundamentally unphilosophic in the formulation of his questions, Socrates is philosophical and sophisticated in the knowledge of what he wants to know. His method is argument and his goal is truth.

That truth will not be found in the customs and beliefs of the multitude. The drama of the latter part of the dialogue consists in the progressive conversion of the common sense position of Protagoras into the philosophic theories of Plato's Socrates. Just as the Presocratics, in their reflections upon nature, transformed popular myths into speculative philosophy, so we here see Socrates undermining accepted moral thought by developing the implications of some of its assumptions and providing a tentative example of the kind of science that must take its place.

But no conclusions are established in the dialogue. This fact, however, has more serious consequences for the way of Protagoras than for that of Socrates. The Sophist's career depends upon results. The lessons he gives to his students are separate and distinct from the life they live in the city. Their encounters with Protagoras are intended to be means to success in that life. Protagoras' teaching, therefore, is ultimately measured by the prosperity it is meant to bring to his students.

For Socrates, there is no distinction between philosophy and life, so that success in inquiry is not measured by something that is extrinsic to it. Socrates is *all* inquirer. His welfare resides in the possession of a mind that is wholly devoted to the pursuit of truth, not in some distillate of inquiry which may be instrumental in bringing about accomplishments in the world. His model, he concludes by telling us, is the Prometheus of Protagoras' myth. "I follow his lead and spend my time on all these matters as a means of taking forethought for my whole life" (361d3–5).

3

The Parmenides as a Turning Point

I. INTRODUCTION

Gilbert Ryle, in the 1963 afterword to his essay, "Plato's *Parmenides*,"[1] written twenty-four years earlier, notes that while Part I of the dialogue is written in indirect discourse, Part II, after its beginning, proceeds entirely in direct discourse. From this he infers that "Plato cannot have composed either Part with the intention that it should be the complement, inside one dialogue, of the other Part" and concludes that his own "attempt in the [1939] article to render the questions canvassed in Part II pertinent to those canvassed in Part I may have been gratuitous."[2]

Ryle should not have given up on the aim of showing the dialogue to be a unified work: the bit of stylistic evidence on which his recantation rests is flimsy compared with the case for unity based on an interpretation of its philosophic substance. In this chapter I propose to make such an attempt, although I will do so by means of a detailed discussion of Part I only. This introductory section will deal in a general way with the second part and with the relation of the two parts to each other.

---

1. *Mind,* N.S. 48 (1939); reprinted in R. E. Allen (ed.), *Studies in Plato's Metaphysics* (London: Routledge & Kegan Paul, 1965). Page references are to the reprinted version.

2. *Ibid.,* p. 145.

The second and longer part of the *Parmenides* relegates Socrates to the role of a mere listener. The company succeeds in persuading Parmenides to give an example of a dialectical exercise and for twenty-nine Stephanus pages the father of Eleatic philosophy develops a series of complex, not to say crabbed, arguments, while Aristoteles, the youngest of those present (who is said to be the one "likely to give the least trouble" [137b6–7][3]) serves as the submissive respondent. The discussion is to be about "those objects which are specially apprehended by discourse and can be regarded as forms" (135e3–4) and, not surprisingly, Parmenides chooses to concern himself with the One, or Unity.[4] Of the eight hypotheses taken up, four assume that the One exists and four that it does not. As the arguments go, however, the conclusions reached by the first and third of each set are then contradicted by those arrived at by the hypotheses immediately following.

Interpretations of these arguments about the One—their validity itself is controversial—have diverged sharply. Neoplatonists have seen them as yielding important metaphysical conclusions, while at least one writer thought them a parody of Eleatic dialectic and "one of the funniest things in philosophy."[5] A less extreme view has seen the eight hypotheses as a dialectical exercise engaged in merely for its own sake; still others have regarded them as mental gymnastics that contain various doctrinal lessons as well. W. G. Runciman, in "Plato's *Parmenides*,"[6] carefully sorts out the major interpretations of this puzzling section and convincingly, if briefly, points up the difficulties that beset each of them.[7]

---

3. Unless otherwise indicated, the Cornford translation of the *Parmenides* is cited: Francis M. Cornford, *Plato and Parmenides* (Library of Liberal Arts 102 [Indianapolis: Bobbs-Merrill, 1957]). Translation cited by permission of Routledge & Kegan Paul Ltd., and Humanities Press, Inc.

4. I shall, in this chapter, capitalize the names of forms.

5. P. H. Frye, as quoted in Cornford, *Plato and Parmenides*, p. 114.

6. *Harvard Studies in Classical Philology*, 64 (1959); reprinted in R. E. Allen, *Studies in Plato's Metaphysics*. Page references are to the reprinted version.

7. *Ibid.*, pp. 167–176. I refer the reader to Runciman's essay for details. More generally, I am indebted to this essay because it led me to see the

Runciman's own account does justice to the "gymnastics" of Parmenides' treatment of the eight hypotheses. After all, the dialogue itself so characterizes the venerable philosopher's performance (135c, d, 136c). In his view, however, there is a point to the exercise beyond the lesson in dialectic it teaches to the young Socrates. "The moral of the exercise is that forms are not definable by deduction from existential hypotheses. Exhaustive application of this method has been shown to lead as legitimately to one set of contradictory conclusions as to the other."[8] But that method—dialectic—is essentially that of "hypothesis and deduction" of the properties of a form[9] which is typical of the dialogues prior to the *Parmenides*. Runciman sees Plato as becoming aware of the limitation of a procedure he had developed out of Socrates' own search for definitions and as coming to realize that definitions of forms "involve statements describing interrelations existing between forms."[10]

No new philosophic method is developed in the *Parmenides*, but it appears at a date not too distant from it. The *Phaedrus*, "where definition is declared necessary to the knowledge of truth,"[11] contains the first announcement of that method, accompanied by expressions of great optimism regarding its fruitfulness. Dialectic is to consist of collection, "in which we bring a dispersed plurality under a single form, seeing it all together: the purpose being to define so-and-so (265d3–4), and of division, "whereby we are enabled to divide into forms, following the objective articulation" (265e1–2). Finally, the new method is put to use in still later works, above all in the *Statesman* and the *Sophist*, where relations holding among forms are explicitly explored.

Parmenides as an important turning point in Plato's philosophic career. I begin with Runciman's account of the dialogue's second part, which I accept on the basis of the arguments he presents. I shall here only summarize his conclusions.

8. *Ibid.*, p. 181.
9. *Ibid.*, p. 182.
10. *Ibid.*, p. 179.
11. At 277b5–8. Runciman, "Plato's *Parmenides*," p. 182.

The picture we here gain is that of a changing conception of what dialectic is, for Plato. He begins with the essentially critical method of the elenchus that is characteristic of those Socratic dialogues in which the pursuit of knowledge is not yet the search for forms. In the middle dialogues, the method of hypothesis comes strongly to the fore,[12] while Plato's last specification of the method by means of which knowledge is to be gained is collection and division. Runciman convincingly shows the second part of the *Parmenides* to be a turning point in this evolution of Plato's method. By having Parmenides demonstrate four principles and their opposites as well, Plato rejects the method of the middle dialogues and the way is prepared for his final attempt to arrive at the truth about forms.

To see how this account can further our understanding of the first part of the dialogue and of the work as a single whole, it will be worthwhile to go somewhat afield by commenting on a text from the *Republic*.

> In the case of a faculty I look to one thing only—that to which it is related and what it effects, and it is in this way that I come to call each one of them a faculty, and that which is related to the same thing and accomplishes the same thing I call the same faculty and that which accomplishes another and relates to another I call other.[13]

That "different faculties are naturally related to different objects"[14] is an expression of a fundamental axiom, not only of Plato's philosophy but of Greek philosophy during its golden period. What there is can be known and what can not be known simply is not; the world is intelligible to the human mind. True, reality is not accessible to men unless they do the work it takes to get to know it; there are no shortcuts. But by way of compensation, there are no patches of unintelligibility

---

12. Although it tends to be more talked about than actually employed. See the discussion in Richard Robinson, *Plato's Earlier Dialectic* (2nd ed.; Oxford: Clarendon Press, 1953), pp. 202–204.

13. *Republic* 477c9–d5.

14. *Republic* 478a12–13.

in the universe, no unknowable, mysterious realities. Some pages after the quoted passages, the conviction that there is complete harmony between the ontological and the epistemic orders is elaborated by means of the simile of the Divided Line.[15] And however much Plato may have changed his views concerning some of the things represented by that heavily burdened line, nowhere does he give us reason to think that he abandoned this parallelism between the modes of apprehension and their objects.

Needless to say, such a parallelism has implications: the mind must be conceived of as *capable* of apprehending its objects and the objects must be understood as *fit* for apprehension by such a mind. We must not try to bail water with a sieve, nor hold fire in a wool sack. Moreover, changes in characterization of one side of the Divided Line require corresponding modifications on the other.

By what "faculty"—the word is *dynamis*—does Plato understand knowledge to be attained? A search for his analysis of the faculty of reason—as if Plato were a nineteenth-century follower of Kant—would be futile. For Plato, that faculty is but the power to know, and little is to be said about it except just how the ability is exercised. In short, its nature is constituted by the method by means of which knowledge is achieved. In its highest mode—that which leads to knowledge unqualified—the method is dialectic. "Dialectic was not a propaedeutic to philosophy. It was not a tool that you might choose to use in philosophizing. It was philosophy itself, the very search for essences, only considered in its methodological aspect. The method occurred only in the search, and the search only by means of the method."[16] If the world is intelligible by its very nature, it is thus *dialectic* which is naturally related to its objects.

If there is a necessary harmony between method and object, then a change in the conception of the one calls for an altera-

15. *Republic* 509d–511e.
16. Robinson, *Plato's Earlier Dialectic,* p. 71.

tion in the understanding of the other. The fact, therefore—
and it is not a matter of controversy—that Plato's conception
of dialectic underwent important changes in the course of his
long career creates a presumption that he modified his conception of the forms as well. We have seen that the method that
is employed in the *Sophist* is not that of the *Phaedo* or
Republic; accordingly, this evidence alone makes it highly
likely that the forms whose interweaving is taken up in the
later dialogue do not have the same characteristics as those of
which the *Republic*'s philosopher-ruler is said to have a vision.

In order of composition, the *Parmenides* stands between the
Phaedo and the *Republic,* on the one hand, and the *Statesman*
and the *Sophist,* on the other.[17] But more important, in the
second part of our dialogue, Plato uses Parmenides to reveal
the inadequacy of the method meant to lead the philosopher
of the *Republic* to a vision of the forms and, by taking up some
questions about the relations among forms, to point forward
to the later conception of dialectic as collection and division.
Now, the first part of the *Parmenides* is entirely devoted to the
theory of forms itself. May it not be that the criticism of the
theory which is there put forward should be understood as an
enterprise of revision, in the course of which Plato begins to
transform his understanding of the forms as they had func-
tioned in the *Phaedo* and *Republic* to that which will hold for
the forms of the *Statesman* and the *Sophist?*

It is the thesis of this chapter that the *Parmenides* is a turning point in a more radical way than Runciman took it to be.[18]

---

17. About this there is well-nigh complete agreement. See David Ross,
Plato's Theory of Ideas (Oxford: Clarendon Press, 1951), pp. 2–10. The
Phaedrus, however, is regarded by some as having been written just before
the *Parmenides* and by others as soon after. This uncertainty is in keeping
with the transitional character of that great dialogue, with its metaphors
of the *vision* of forms in its first part and the introduction of the method
of collection and division toward its end.

18. Runciman's own view is that Plato takes the arguments he has
Parmenides make against the forms as raising serious difficulties; but, since
Plato continues to believe in forms in his later dialogues, Plato is not
regarded as considering those difficulties insurmountable. See his "Plato's
Parmenides," pp. 149–161.

The theory of forms, there, does not remain untouched nor is it abandoned.[19] Instead, a detailed consideration of the text of the first part of the *Parmenides* will show that in this dialogue, Plato begins a revision of his conception of the forms. However, just as in Part II of the *Parmenides* Plato neither formulates nor uses the new method (but merely makes an elaborate sketch by way of progress toward it), so he refrains, in Part I, from making explicit a revised theory of forms. Rather, he prepares the way for such a theory by producing arguments designed to purge the conception of forms of characteristics that are now unwanted.[20]

II. THE OPENING (126a–130b)

"After leaving our home at Clazomenae . . ." (126a1); an otherwise unknown Cephalus and some friends have come to Athens specifically to hear a recital of the discussion Socrates had had long ago with Zeno and Parmenides. Cephalus and his unnamed companions meet with Glaucon and Adeimantus, who take them to the home of their half brother, Antiphon. Antiphon's life is now devoted to horses, but when he was young he had often heard an account of the conversation from Zeno's friend, Pythodorus, who had himself been a witness to the encounter. Antiphon is reluctant to repeat the conversation and understandably declares it to be "no easy matter" (127a6); but he obliges his half brothers and their friends and tells the long and complex tale.

The confrontation of Socrates with Zeno and Parmenides had taken place long ago. By having the report come down to us thrice removed from the event—Pythodorus told Antiphon

---

19. The only alternatives Runciman considers. *Ibid.*

20. Among recent interpretations which bear some resemblance to mine are those of Herman L. Sinaiko in Ch. 4 of his *Love, Knowledge, and Discourse: Dialogue and Dialectic in Phaedrus, Republic, Parmenides* (Chicago: University of Chicago Press, 1965) and J. M. E. Moravcsik in "The 'Third Man' Argument and Plato's Theory of Forms," *Phronesis,* 8 (1963).

who told Cephalus—Plato, whose characters they here are, gives a mythic quality to the conversation: in fact, no such meeting has ever taken place at all. The means, however, by which Plato makes the discussion legendary have their positive significance as well. The very opening lines of the *Parmenides* establish a continuity with the *Republic*. Glaucon and Adeimantus are two major interlocutors of Socrates in the earlier dialogue, and its reporter to us is a namesake of the old gentleman who there offers the first definition of justice. The conversation with Parmenides about to be narrated is concerned with forms and dialectic, with the objects of knowledge and the method which attains them. Plato wants to be sure that his readers bear in mind what he had said about them in his earlier works.

Plato's own dialectic is a development of the questioning to which Socrates had subjected those with whom he philosophized in the agora, and his theory of forms is in part an attempt to make good Socrates' search for objectivity. In earlier dialogues, Plato had examined other men's views regarding knowledge and found them wanting: the speechifying and relativism of leading Sophists,[21] the word-mongering of Cratylus,[22] and the frivolous and anti-philosophic eristic of Euthydemus and his brother.[23] In the *Phaedo,* the assignment of particular efficient causes of various phenomena by that "branch of learning which is called natural science"[24] is dismissed as not making the world intelligible, and so is the more sophisticated nature philosophy of Anaxagoras who "adduced causes like air and aether and water and many other absurdities."[25] This rejection (and the *Phaedo*) is recalled by the

---

21. In the *Gorgias,* for example, and the *Protagoras.* See Ch. 2 for a discussion of the latter.
22. In the dialogue of that name. See Ch. 1, above.
23. In the *Euthydemus.*
24. *Phaedo* 96a7–8.
25. *Phaedo* 98b9–c2.

first words of our dialogue, where Clazomenae, the home of
Anaxagoras, is mentioned.[26] But in the *Meno,* the *Phaedo,*
and, above all, in the *Republic,* Plato had gone far beyond the
criticism of others, on the one hand, and a depiction of
Socratic questioning, on the other, to develop positive views
as well. To a large extent, however, Plato's account of forms
had proceeded by way of similes, and concerning the dialectic which leads to the forms' apprehension, he found himself unable to give much of an explicit analysis.[27] He now
turns to the Eleatics for assistance in bringing to the surface
what had remained implicit and in revising what had come to
seem inadequate.

But help is not to come from Zeno: Plato prefers to go back
to the originator of Eleatic philosophy rather than to continue
in the direction taken by his pupil. At the beginning of
Antiphon's account, Zeno is just completing the reading of a
treatise. With great artistic skill (in a dialogue that otherwise
cares little for artistry), Plato repudiates the Zenonian version
of the Eleatic method.[28] "Zeno was nearing forty" (127b4),
the age at which it is classically declared *"floruit!"* but the
book he reads from is not of recent composition; apparently
he has had nothing to say since his youthful work. Nor does
Zeno's essay contribute something new to philosophy: it
attempts to refute the attackers of Parmenides' monism by deriving paradoxes from the pluralism *they* maintain. And
finally, Plato has Pythodorus and Parmenides absent themselves while Zeno reads (127c); they have heard it all before.

---

26. With regard to the problems that interested him, Plato was as
aware of his predecessors and contemporaries as Aristotle. Characteristically, however, his historical interest does not take systematic form.

27. *Republic* 533a.

28. I am largely indebted to Robert S. Brumbaugh (*Plato on the One:
The Hypotheses in the Parmenides* [New Haven: Yale University Press,
1961], pp. 30–31) for pointing out how unflattering the treatment of Zeno
is.

Plato does not intend to lean on a form of Eleatic dialectic that is by its nature merely negative in its aim: it stands in the service of the enterprise of refuting. Accordingly, when in a short while Parmenides too engages in criticism, we know that he is to be taken with utter seriousness.

After Zeno has finished reading, Socrates asks him to repeat his very first argument and then proceeds to launch into a vigorous critique of it. "If things are many," Zeno maintains, "they must be both like and unlike" (127e6–8). But since this is impossible, it cannot be that there is a plurality at all.[29] No difficulty is raised, Socrates responds, if one recognizes that there are such things as forms and notes that forms and the things that participate in them are different in regard to the issue Zeno raises. A form cannot possess contrary properties: the form of Like cannot be Unlike; if *that* could be shown, says Socrates, "I should be filled with admiration" (129e5). But that ordinary things should have contrary properties is no more remarkable than that Socrates should be one person (and thus partake of Unity) and yet have many different parts (and so participate in Plurality).

Before this dialogue, Plato's leading character had been a mature Socrates: here it is a young and impetuous Socrates who makes these criticisms. Pythodorus, Zeno, and Parmenides exchange glances and smile as he talks, proud of him in an almost fatherly way. When Parmenides now asks his first question, it is clear why it can never be answered. "Have you yourself drawn this distinction you speak of and separated apart on the one side forms themselves and on the other the things that share in them?" (130b1–3). No young Socrates ever made such a distinction, nor was there anyone from whom he might

---

29. Following Cornford, this should be understood as follows: if there are many things in the world, they must, since they all *are*, be all homogeneous. However, since they are distinguishably *many*, they must be heterogeneous as well. See Cornford, *Plato and Parmenides*, p. 68.

have learned it. The Socrates of this dialogue is pointedly made fictional: the young Socrates and the old Parmenides together are Plato himself in the process of being reborn. What Plato has had Socrates say about the forms up to this point must be reconsidered in the light of a more rigorous Parmenidean logic. We must go to prior works for an understanding of the present object of controversy.

The forms figure more or less importantly in at least four pre-*Parmenides* dialogues: the *Meno*, the *Cratylus*, the *Phaedo,* and the *Republic.* In their commentary on the last-named work, R. C. Cross and A. D. Woozley ably summarize the various functions Plato has had the forms perform in these middle dialogues.[30] I shall borrow from them and summarize their summary. (*1*) The forms are the objects of knowledge, contrasting with what we perceive, the objects of belief.[31] (*2*) The forms alone *are;* their true reality contrasts with the lesser reality of the world of becoming or change.[32] (*3*) The forms serve as ideal standards for the particulars of the familiar world. They are perfect in a way these particulars can only approximate.[33] (*4*) The forms are universals. They account for the fact that we can apply the same general name to many different particulars.[34] (*5*) The forms are causes (*aitiâ*); because of them, the particulars we perceive have the characteristics which they have.[35]

---

30. R. C. Cross and A. D .Woozley, *Plato's Republic: A Philosophical Commentary* (London: Macmillan, 1964), pp. 180–183. Also see H. F. Cherniss, "The Philosophical Economy of the Theory of Ideas," *The American Journal of Philology,* 57 (1936); reprinted in Allen, *Studies in Plato's Metaphysics.* This paper is discussed by Cross and Woozley, pp. 183–195. See Moravcsik, "The 'Third Man' Argument," *Phronesis,* for a somewhat different list of five "conceptions" of forms.

31. E.g., *Republic* 474b–480a.

32. E.g., *Republic* 476e–477a.

33. E.g., *Cratylus* 389a–b; *Phaedo* 74a–75d; *Republic* 474b–480a, 596b–597e.

34. E.g., *Meno* 72a–75a; *Republic* 596a.

35. *Phaedo* 100c–d, especially.

Nowhere in the middle dialogues—and this has often been noted before—does the theory of forms properly become the center of discussion. Indeed, the topic of the forms is never even introduced for its own sake: discussion of the forms is always limited by the requirements of some *other* problem, such as the immortality of the soul or the nature of the philosopher-ruler. In the *Parmenides,* for the first time, the theory of forms moves to the center of the stage and is discussed for itself. Between the completion of the *Republic* and the writing of the *Parmenides* Plato must have reflected on how he used the forms in his more recent work. Specifically, he must have come to realize that one and the same class of entities could not perform all the functions that had been assigned to the forms in different contexts. There is tension between what are essentially two different conceptions of forms, though we must remain aware of the fact that up until now such conceptions have remained inchoate. On one side there are exemplars: standards possessing the highest value and maximal reality and having a certain creative causal power—that is, functions (*2*), (*3*), and (*5*). On the other side are forms that are universals or principles: they are meanings which make language possible—that is, function (*4*). In both views—call one metaphysical and the other logical—the forms remain the highest object of knowledge (*1*), though they are this in ways that differ importantly from each other.

The arguments that begin at *Parmenides* 130b are designed to show that the exemplar-conception of forms must be abandoned in favor of the view which has them fulfilling the function of universals or, possibly, that there must be two distinct conceptions of forms.[36] We then see that just as Plato is now preparing to develop a new method in philosophy, so he also lays the groundwork for a revision of his account of the forms.

---

36. Here only a general statement of this sort is possible; a more precise (and less apodictic) account of the forms will be given in the course of a treatment of the arguments of the *Parmenides.*

Parmenides takes over from Zeno and Socrates is put on the
defensive.

III. The Extent of the Realm
of Forms (130b-c)

This first interchange establishes the revisionist theme of the
entire set of arguments.[37] On being questioned by Parmenides, Socrates is confident of the existence of such forms
as Likeness, Unity, and Plurality, as well as of such forms as
Rightness, Beauty, and Goodness (130b). He is puzzled by the
question as to whether there are forms of Man, Fire, and
Water (130c) and completely perplexed as to whether he
should admit such forms as Hair, Mud, or Dirt.

The first sort of forms—call them metaphysical or mathe-
matical and forms of values—are posited most frequently in
prior dialogues. Forms of this kind spring most immediately
out of the historical Socrates' own concerns, as he attempts to
find objective answers to ethical questions, and they have the
advantage of familiarity. Moreover, they fail to be problematic, for both Socrates and the reader who has been following Plato up to the present dialogue, because their great
abstractness successfully hides whatever conflict there might
be between their roles as exemplars and as universals. The
next set of putative forms is much less discussed in earlier
works, and the fact that these forms are forms of physical objects makes the tension between the metaphysical and the logical functions of the forms more manifest. Nevertheless, Socrates says only that he has "often been puzzled about those
things" (130c3–4). Man, as the most important of all species,
and Fire and Water, as two of the elements from which all

---

37. Little attention has been paid to this passage, but see Julius
Stenzel, *Plato's Method of Dialectic,* trans. and ed. D. J. Allan (Oxford:
Clarendon Press, 1940), pp. 54ff.

things are made, have such strong claims to be included in the realm of forms that Socrates is not yet prepared to question their legitimacy as forms.

But when, finally, we descend to Hair, Mud, and Dirt, all such prima facie claims for admission to the realm of forms fall away. As soon as forms of such lowly things are mentioned, a problem that is implicit for all forms becomes explicit.

Hair, Mud, and Dirt. These things, says Socrates, "are just the things we see; it would surely be too absurd to suppose they have a form" (130d3–5). Mud is to wallow in; what place could it possibly have in the topmost portion of the Divided Line? If forms have maximal reality, Muddiness will be far more real than the most accurately fashioned model of a tetrahedron. And will Dirt itself not be more valuable than Socrates, who was in his time "the bravest and also the wisest and most upright man"?[38] There seems thus to be very good ground for *excluding* these "undignified objects" (130c6) from the realm of forms.

Yet, however absurd it may be to have forms of the likes of Mud, Socrates is immediately compelled to reconsider. He confesses that he has "sometimes been troubled by a doubt whether what is true in one case may not be true in all" (130d). And he is surely right if we posit "a single idea or form in the case of the various multiplicities to which we give the same name."[39] On such grounds, there is no more reason to rule out a form of Hair or Mud than of Justice or Unity, for in all such cases we give the same name to many individual instances. The relation of universal to instance holds for trivial things just as it does for important things: the problem of the one in the many must be solved for all classes. Immediately Socrates is "driven to retreat, for fear of tumbling into a bottomless pit of nonsense" (130d6–7). For it would indeed

---

38. *Phaedo* 118a16–17.
39. *Republic* 596a6–7.

be nonsense to suppose that all the things that are "just the things we see" (130d3–4) should have a place in the direct light of the sun.

Socrates' rapid vacillation, within a short paragraph, between the two conceptions of the forms exhibits well the tension between them. Parmenides, at the same time, is sanguine about the ultimate outcome. He expects that Socrates will resolve the issue when he is less young and immature. A moment earlier he had praised Socrates: "Your eagerness for discussion is admirable" (130b1). But now he adds that "philosophy has not yet taken hold of you so firmly as I believe it will some day" (130e2–3). This contrast between youth and maturity is echoed only five pages later in the transitional passage to the second portion of the dialogue. There, youth is identified with a "passion for argument" (135d2–3) that remains in important ways untutored; right now, Socrates lacks "preliminary training" (135d1). Maturity comes with the "severer training in what the world calls idle talk and condemns as useless" (135d4–5). Then (as now), much of the world looked askance at the pursuit of logic or the sort of analysis to be found in the second part of the *Parmenides*. "At present," Parmenides says to Socrates, "your youth makes you still pay attention to what the world will think" (130e3–4). Later, however, he will come to see that

> if . . . a man refuses to admit that forms of things exist or to distinguish a definite form in every case (eidos henos hekastou), he will have nothing on which to fix his thought, so long as he will not allow that each thing has a character which is always the same, and in so doing he will completely destroy the significance of all discourse (135b5–c2).

In short, maturing is a matter of learning dialectic and recognizing the need for forms that can fulfill the role of universals.

A consequence of this demand upon the forms is that the realm of forms must be sufficiently extensive to include forms of whatever may enter into discourse. But then—and this is the lesson of this first interchange between Parmenides and Socrates—forms cannot be valuable in the way in which, say, the philosophic life is valuable by contrast to that of the tyrant. The forms' value must attach solely to their being the ground of intelligibility and the objects of the highest sort of knowledge, but in no way to the specific natures of those objects. And the form of Mud forces an analogous observation about reality. The notion that there is a straightforward increase in reality, from dream objects and shadows to the forms, must ultimately be replaced by a more complex distinguishing into *kinds* of reality. If, for the sake of discourse and knowledge, there is to be a form of Mud, it will not do to say that it is more real, *simpliciter,* than, for example, the Parthenon. Instead, it can only be seen as real in a different way. No new view, of course, is given in this passage: only a clearing of the path toward such a one has been begun.

IV. Sharing (131a-e)

"You say you hold that there exist certain forms, of which these other things come to partake and so to be called after their names?" (130e5–131a1). When Socrates assents, Parmenides begins to press him on the difficult question of partaking. He wonders how a "form as a whole, a single thing, is in each of the many" particulars which partake of it (131a8–9), for it would seem that "a form which is one and the same will be at the same time as a whole, in a number of things which are separate, and consequently will be separate from itself" (131b1–2). Socrates is not at all fazed by this challenge and responds immediately. Mindful of the *logical* function of the forms, Socrates offers an analogy which appears to solve the problem of the one and the many: "One and the same day . . . is in many places at the same time and nevertheless is not separate from itself. Suppose any given form is in them all at

the same time as one and the same thing in that way"
(131b3–6).

But it is easy to push the untrained Socrates back to the
metaphysical conception. "I like the way you make out that
one and the same thing is in many places at once" (131b7–8),
admits Parmenides and promptly substitutes the fatal analogy
of the sail: "You might as well spread a sail over a number of
people and then say that the one sail as a whole was over them
all" (131b8–9). Knowing full well that Socrates has not yet
learned the lesson of the previous argument, he now taunts
him by asking "Don't you think that is a fair analogy?"
(131b9)[40] and exacts a hesitant assent.

But of course it is not fair. If the day were regarded as con-
sisting of the sun's rays, rays that are absorbed by him on
whom they shine, only then would you and I partake of the
same day precisely as we might share a sail covering us. Yet
surely this is not how we normally think of a day: this attempt
by Socrates to find a model for the relation of partaking, however difficult it might have been to work out, is never even
begun. Plato's purpose here is limited to criticism: Parmenides
shifts to the simple but unusable relation of physical sharing.

Nevertheless, the substitution of the sail is not frivolous toy-
ing with Socrates' confusion. In the previous argument, where
the issue was the extent of the realm of forms, a tension was
revealed between two ways of regarding the forms. Now, however, Parmenides begins to uncover a fundamental difficulty
that besets the metaphysical conception. So that everything
that has a certain characteristic may have a share in the
appropriate form, "the forms themselves must be divisible into
parts, and the things which have a share in them will have a
part for their share" (131c5–7). A marvelous bundle of absurdities can now be drawn from this axiom. When Largeness is
divided up, then "each of the many large things is to be large

---

40. Or, more literally, "Don't you think you are saying some such
thing?"

by virtue of a part of Largeness which is smaller than Largeness itself" (131c12–d2); when it is Equality that is sliced into parts, something is made equal to something else by a portion of the form which is less than Equality itself. Finally, the smallness that is to be found in some small thing will be smaller than the form of Smallness itself!

Participation or partaking or sharing is treated in the most naive way. It is almost an exaggeration to speak of an analogy between forms and physical objects: there appears to be no difference at all between the cutting up of forms and the slicing of pies into portions. As they reject the various silly conclusions about Largeness, Equality, and Smallness, Plato has Parmenides and Socrates most emphatically repudiate a conception of forms that makes them quasi-physical in character.

A whole sail, as well as the piece of a sail which might cover me, is sail-ish; that is, both whole and part have sail qualities. The argument under consideration leads to an absurd conclusion precisely because it is expected that both Largeness and large things should be large and that Smallness and small things should be small. (What is amusingly horrible about the outcome is that Largeness should turn out to be small rather than large, and so on.) The analogy of the sail implies literal self-predication,[41] that is, "that the Form corresponding to a given character itself has that character."[42]

We might say at this point that Plato disposes of self-predication at the same time that he disposes of the analogy

---

41. The term "self-predication" was introduced by Professor Gregory Vlastos in his seminal "The Third Man Argument in the *Parmenides*," *Philosophical Review*, 63 (1954), reprinted in Allen, *Studies in Plato's Metaphysics*. Henceforth this essay will be referred to as *Vlastos, 1954*, and the page numbers of the reprinted version will be used.

42. Gregory Vlastos, " 'Self-Predication' in Plato's Later Period," *Philosophical Review*, 78 (1969), 74, subsequently to be referred to as *Vlastos, 1969a*. To avoid giving the impression that besides forms and instances of them there should be an additional character, it might be better to say that in self-prediction the character—imperfectly belonging to things in the physical world—which is named by the name of the form is predicated of the form.

of forms to physical objects, since self-predication obviously holds for such entities. (If Largeness is like a very large thing, then surely it is large!) But just because self-predication is here tied so intimately to forms that are hardly distinguished from physical objects, the issue of self-predication *tout simple* cannot be considered as settled. A less literal and less univocal interpretation remains open.

The issue of self-predication is central to the aims of this first part of the *Parmenides* because it is central to the metaphysical conception of the forms. Plato is not using Parmenides to refute the views of others,[43] but is clarifying his *own* mind about the nature of forms, making revisions in the process. To be sure, it is not clear how aware Plato was, prior to this point, that he was assuming self-predication to hold for the forms,[44] but the views expressed in the *Phaedo* and the *Republic* do in any case commit him to that assumption.[45]

First, if forms are exemplary causes, as is explicitly maintained in the passage beginning at *Phaedo* 100c, self-predication of some sort is called for. Socrates is unhappy with an account that explains "why a given object is beautiful" by saying that "it has a gorgeous color or shape or any such attribute"[46] and with a statement that asserts that "one man is taller than another by a head."[47] The difference in character between cause and effect makes such accounts unsatisfactory:

---

43. As was held, for example, by A. E. Taylor. See his *Plato: The Man and His Work* (New York: Meridian reprint of the 6th ed., 1956), pp. 349–351.

44. R. S. Bluck thinks that he was "at least to some extent conscious of this assumption that he was making." See his "The *Parmenides* and the 'Third Man,'" *Classical Quarterly*, n.s., 6 (1956), 30.

45. In my view, the one instance in which Plato's language appears to explicitly attribute the character that is named by the name of a form *to* that form—namely, *Protagoras* 330c–e, where justice is said to be just and holiness to be holy—*should* be read as an inchoate view of forms as self-predicative. (See pp. 69–72, above.) The case to be made here, however, does not rely on this controversial passage; it does, however, lean heavily on the discussion of self-predication in *Vlastos, 1954*, pp. 244–254.

46. *Phaedo* 100c10–d2.

47. *Phaedo* 100e8–9.

it is Beauty that makes objects beautiful and Tallness that makes men tall. Like causes like.

Second, in the view exhibited by the Divided Line and confirmed both by the Allegory of the Cave and by the discussion of art in Book X of the *Republic,*[48] there is an ascent in degree of reality as one goes from a lower to a higher section of the Line. Plato means to do justice both to Parmenides and to Heracleitus by affirming the reality of the unchanging and of the flux. His aim, however, is clearly not to posit two separate worlds, a sharp dualism, that is, of being and becoming. But the avoidance of such a chasm between two realms requires that some one thing become more real as one moves to the higher sections of the Divided Line, that a continuous road lead from the cave to the sun. And what persists are the characteristics—being equal or being just, etc.—which are successively the objects of delusion, of belief, of discursive knowledge, and of intellectual vision, precisely because they are successively more real.

Finally, that the doctrine which ascribes degrees to reality calls for self-predication can be seen with particular clarity when one recognizes that with an increase in reality also comes an increase in value. If the representation of a bed is less a bed than an actual bed, is not the form of Bed, by extension, still more a bed than the bed we sleep in? Does Plato not insist that the form of Beauty is more beautiful than any beautiful object?[49] The forms stand at the apex of the edifice: if we do not say that the form of Bed is perfectly a bed and the form of Beauty perfectly beautiful, to what else, according to the sort of view that is conveyed in the *Republic,* could such perfection be attributed?

I have stated flatly that by the time Plato had completed the *Republic* he was fully committed to the self-predication assumption. Still, this way of talking is somewhat misleading.

---

48. *Republic* 509d–517a, 595a–598c.
49. See *Phaedrus* 249d–250d, for example.

Similes, allegories, metaphors do not, strictly speaking, entail assumptions. And since by their means the theory of forms is conveyed rather than stated, no self-predication assumption is either asserted by Plato in so many words nor is one logically compelled to assume it by what Plato does say about forms. Nevertheless, only by means of the self-predication assumption can this aspect of what Plato says about the forms be made coherent; it provides much the most natural and straightforward way of spelling out what is given in the dialogues before the *Parmenides*. The *Parmenides* itself shows that Plato became aware of his commitment and was troubled by it.

V. PARTICIPATION: THIRD MAN ARGUMENT, FIRST VERSION (132a-b)

On the supposition that the objects of the physical world participate in forms, the Third Man Argument (TMA), with which Parmenides confronts the struggling Socrates, proposes to show that an unacceptable regress inevitably follows:

> (*i*) *Whenever you think that a certain number of things are large you perhaps think that there exists a certain one Form, the same in your view of all of them; hence you believe that the one thing, Largeness, exists.* . . . (*ii*) *What then if you view in your mind Largeness itself and the other large things?* (*iii*) *Will not another Largeness show up, in virtue of which all these will appear large?* . . . *So another form of Largeness will come into view, over and above Largeness and its participants.*[50] (*iv*) *And again,*

---

50. *Parmenides* 132a2–11, translated by Gregory Vlastos in his "Plato's Third Man Argument," *Philosophical Quarterly,* 19 (1969), 290–291, henceforth referred to as *Vlastos, 1969b.* The added roman numbers will be useful for quick reference.

covering all these, yet another, which will make all of them large. So each of your forms will no longer be one, but an indefinite number.[51]

Our starting point is the Vlastos analysis of the TMA.[52] According to it, a rigorous formulation of the argument requires the insertion of two premises that are not made explicit in the text, and it reveals, moreover, that the two tacit premises, together with one of the explicit ones, yield a contradiction. On this reading, then, the TMA may be formulated as follows:[53]

1.1. If *a, b,* and *c,* etc., are *F,* then there exists a unique form, *F*-ness, such that *a, b,* and *c,* etc., are *F* by participating in that *F*-ness.

1.2. *a, b,* and *c* are *F.*

SP. *F*-ness is *F.*

1.3. *a, b, c,* and *F*-ness are *F.*

NI. If *x* is *F* by participating in *F*-ness, then $x \neq F$-ness.

1.4. Therefore, there exists a unique form, *F*-ness *II,* such that *a, b, c,* and *F*-ness are *F* by participating in *F*-ness *II.*

---

51. *Parmenides* 132a11–b2, in the Cornford translation.

52. Any discussion of the TMA must begin with Vlastos' essay of 1954, as elaborated and refined by *Vlastos, 1969b*. While the TMA has intrigued philosophers since Aristotle and has been widely discussed (a selected bibliography is given in *Vlastos, 1954*, p. 231, n. 2), in the time since Vlastos first brought a particularly potent combination of philosophic and scholarly rigor to the argument, an entirely new and "still-rising flood of literature" has come to be devoted to it. With the quoted phrase, H. F. Cherniss does not mean to be approving of the literature's logical rigor. See his "The Relation of the *Timaeus* to Plato's Later Dialogues," *American Journal of Philology,* 78 (1957); reprinted in Allen, *Studies in Plato's Metaphysics,* p. 369. Most of the recent papers on the TMA are cited in *Vlastos, 1969b*, p. 297, n. 2.

53. I am following the more careful mode of phrasing of *Vlastos, 1969b*, although I am presenting the argument somewhat differently in order to facilitate subsequent comparisons. I do not believe that these modifications affect the substance of the argument.

An indefinite number of additional forms can be derived by iteration of the reasoning.

Let me comment briefly on each step. *1.1* formulates, in generalized form, what Parmenides asserts in *i*. *1.2* simply asserts what is believed by all hands: that some things (more than one) have the same characteristic (e.g, are large). *1.3* restates *ii*, but in such a way as to make explicit that each member of the entire group there named—large things and Largeness— is large. This step, necessary if the conclusion is to be reached, requires the additional premise *SP* (for self-predication). *1.4* formulates *iii*, though not as an interrogative, of course. But this conclusion cannot be obtained without a non-identity assumption *NI* which prevents *F*-ness from being *F* by participating in itself. This second tacit premise simply asserts that if anything has a characteristic by virtue of the fact that it participates in a form, that thing cannot be the form itself.[54]

This, then, is the TMA made fully explicit; its incoherence can be shown as follows:
Given that

> *a*, *b*, and *c* are *F* by participating in a unique form, *F*-ness (*1.1* and *1.2*),

and given that

> *F*-ness is itself *F* (*SP*),

one cannot grant *NI*, since according to it,

> No *x* that is *F* is identical with *F*-ness (*NI*),

"for it would then follow that the form (*F*-ness) cannot be identical with itself."[55]

---

54. Both *Vlastos, 1954* and *Vlastos, 1969b* show in greater detail how *SP* and *NI* are needed for the TMA. The role of the non-identity assumption in the theory of forms generally and in the first part of the *Parmenides* in particular will be taken up in Secs. VI and VII, below.

55. *Vlastos, 1969b*, p. 292. This entire account is a paraphrase of the argument there given. Also see n. 63 below.

In his 1954 paper Vlastos regards Plato as thoroughly puzzled by the TMA, and in none of the papers in which he returns to this topic does he change his views.

> *We can now see why Plato could neither convince himself that
> the Third Man Argument was valid, nor refute it convincingly.
> He could do neither without stating explicitly its two implicit
> assumptions. This he never did: he never looked at either of
> them in the clear light of explicit assertion, for, had he done so,
> he would have compelling reason to repudiate both, since their
> logical consequences are intolerable to a rational mind.*[56]

Vlastos concludes that the TMA is "the record of honest perplexity."[57] At most, it is a partial awakening on Plato's part to
the problems that beset his account of forms. Vlastos does not
see the TMA as a sign of a revision of his theory.

The question of the argument's validity is clearly at the
center of the larger problem of interpretation. It is thus not
surprising that in response to Vlastos at least two formulations
of the TMA were put forward which see the regress as validly
deducible.[58] And if the unacceptable conclusion could be
validly derived, the road would be open to an interpretation
of the TMA which has Plato rejecting a position that is contained in the premises of the argument. In detail, the formulations of Wilfrid Sellars and Colin Strang differ considerably
from each other and from that of Vlastos, but both agree that
something like the self-predication and non-identity assumptions are implicit in the argument. At the same time, however,
both call for a significant revision of what is Vlastos' first
premise (*1.1*). Instead of having Parmenides assert that "there
exists a *unique* form *F*-ness," they read the text as being open
to the interpretation that "there exists *at least one* form,

---

56. *Vlastos, 1954,* p. 254.
57. *Ibid.*
58. Wilfred Sellars, "Vlastos and 'The Third Man,'" *Philosophical
Review,* 64 (1955), and Colin Strang, "Plato and the Third Man," *Proceedings of the Aristotelian Society,* Suppl. vol. 37 (1963).

F-ness."[59] And if this weaker claim is substituted for the second conjunct of *1.1*, what Parmenides says, together with the needed *SP* and *NI*, no longer yields a contradiction. Given the premises, the conclusion follows unproblematically.

However attractive it may be, such a reading cannot be supported. In a detailed examination of the text, Vlastos shows convincingly that "at least one form" cannot be substituted for what he translates as "unique form."[60] He not only demonstrates that Parmenides repeatedly insists on a *single* form, but shows how this interpretation is corroborated by other passages in Plato. In short, no other reading besides that of "just one" is possible: the TMA cannot be reconstructed as valid along the lines that Sellars and Strang suggest. Before leaving this approach, however, I should like to add a comment of a more general sort.

Suppose "at least one form" were a possible reading of the text, what purpose could it have served Plato to build his argument on such a premise? There seem but three possible goals a TMA so reconstructed might have fulfilled. Either (*1*) Plato meant to reject the theory of forms, or (*2*) he meant to criticize a misinterpretation of his theory by showing how a difficulty arises if it is understood in a certain way, or (*3*) he meant to revise his theory of forms by deducing an unacceptable conclusion from a proposition which he once did, but now no longer wishes to, hold.

Each of these alternatives, however, calls for the assumption that at some time Plato himself held the forms to be non-unique or at least that a contemporary believed him to have taken this position. But there is no reason to think that Plato thought of his forms as other than unique. Not only is there an

---

59. I am grossly oversimplifying the two quite different reconstructions of Sellars and Strang. Their papers should be consulted, as well as the debate between Sellars and Vlastos. (See *Vlastos, 1969b*, p. 297, n. 2, for references.)

60. ἓν ἕκαστόν σοι τῶν εἰδῶν ἔσται (132b2). See *Vlastos 1969b* for a painstaking analysis of this and related passages.

explicit passage which insists on uniqueness,[61] but just about none of the functions which the forms were designed to perform could be carried out if the doctrine of forms made it possible for there to be more than one form per characteristic. Nor do I know of any evidence that lends credence to the supposition that some other member of the Academy, say, understood Plato to take the forms to be other than unique. And if this is right, the substitution of the "at least one form" premise would render the TMA pointless. Either (1) Plato is rejecting a theory that he did not and would not hold or (2) a premise would be denied which no contemporary interpreter of Plato had ever asserted or (3) a theory would be revised which had not been maintained by its author. In short, even if the text left one completely free to read it as saying either that there is a unique form or that there is at least one, we should have no warrant to pick the latter. And if, contrary to *anyone*'s claim, we were *required* by the text to translate "at least one form," the place of the TMA in Plato's *oeuvre* would be unlocatable.

The problematic character of the TMA can thus not be eliminated via a rereading of the initial premise; the question thus remains open as to whether the argument is aimed at a particular proposition or whether it simply reflects Plato's confusion. I do not believe that in the TMA Plato records his "honest perplexity" and should like to support this by developing two different, though connected, considerations about the argument.

My first point rests on the thesis that whether or not Plato was puzzled by the TMA depends upon what he *thought* about the argument and not necessarily on what is true of it. Perplexity is a state of mind and derives from belief rather than truth: only if we hold that Plato could not decide whether or not his argument was acceptable do we have grounds for thinking that he was confused. If this is not so, Plato either

---

61. *Republic* 597c. See Strang's discussion, "Plato and the Third Man," pp. 156–157, as well as *Vlastos, 1969b*.

held that the argument he put into Parmenides' mouth reached its conclusion legitimately or that it did not. If we take the latter to be the case, we can only conclude that Plato used the TMA to exhibit as unwarranted some criticism that *others* had made of his theory of forms. If, however, we suppose that Plato thought the TMA to be free of logical problems (so that he could not be said to be perplexed, whatever may in fact be true of the TMA), several interpretations regarding the point of the argument remain open. The TMA might be intended to dispose of the theory of forms altogether or it might be directed merely against some aspect of the theory, as it is expressed in one of the TMA's premises. And whichever one of these is taken to be correct, the argument can be regarded as *self*-criticism and thus seen as attacking a position that Plato himself had previously maintained or as a criticism of an interpretation that *others* had made of his theory of forms. While the question as to whether Plato himself took the argument to be valid thus does not permit us to choose among these various possibilities, it is of vital importance as a preliminary step to such a choice. Accordingly, not only must the question of the argument's validity be carefully considered, but the issue of Plato's own view of that question must be taken up as well.

Why is the TMA—given the Vlastos formulation—a dubious argument? Note that it is not invalid, for the conclusion follows from the premises. But from incompatible premises (*1.1* and *1.2, SP, NI*), anything whatsoever follows, since any given conclusion is but one of infinitely many possible ones. The conclusion of the TMA is thus in no way forced upon us.

A reasonable case can, I believe, be made that Plato did not recognize that his Parmenides' conclusion was derived from premises that are incompatible. To begin with, not all the premises of the argument are explicitly stated. While I believe that Plato was committed to *SP* and to something like *NI*[62] and, in addition, that by the time he wrote the *Parmenides* he

---

62. See Secs. VI and VII.

was aware of that commitment, it is nonetheless difficult to catch a contradiction if the propositions involved are not fully laid out on the table. Moreover, three—not just two—of the argument's premises are needed to yield the contradiction, a fact which further obscures that which makes the TMA questionable.[63] On the grounds, then, that the argument is, after all, valid and that that characteristic which mars it is extremely difficult to see, I think it to be a reasonable supposition that Plato took the premises of the TMA to compel its conclusion.

But perhaps Plato *did* see that the premises of the TMA contained a contradiction; nevertheless, he might have thought that the conclusion which followed from them was perfectly compelling. It was another millennium and a half after the *Parmenides,* in the later Middle Ages, before it became known that from contradictory premises any proposition can be derived.[64] Why then should Plato have supposed the contradiction to undermine the conclusion?

Two objections might be raised against this. First, it may be fairly stated that philosophers and others have often *used* logical principles long before someone was able to state them explicitly. Just as M. Jourdain had been speaking prose long before he discovered this startling fact, *modus ponens* was in use before that principle of inference was isolated. The history

---

63. Even when Vlastos originally discovered the incompatibility of TMA's premises, he thought only two premises were involved (*Vlastos, 1954,* pp. 237–238). It took a few more years before it became clear that three premises were needed. See *Vlastos, 1969b,* especially p. 300, n. 39, where it is pointed out that "the contradiction between *SP* and *NI* could not arise if, for intsance, *F*-ness could be *F* by participating in some Form other than *F*-ness corresponding to *F*, as well it might, were it not for the provision [in *1.1*] that the Form corresponding to *F* is unique."

64. A proof of the theorem which we now express as "$(p \& - p) \supset q$" is found in a work that is included in the 1639 edition of the writings of Duns Scotus (1266–1308); it is now, however, attributed to a Pseudo-Scot. See William and Mary Kneale, *The Development of Logic* (Oxford: Clarendon Press, 1962), pp. 242, 281ff.

of logic does not run parallel to the history of reasoning. Nevertheless, I am not at all sure that this fact constitutes a valid objection here. The present case is an argument in which the conclusion *does* validly follow from the premises, so that to become puzzled by the argument and to reject the conclusion requires *more* than the ability to *employ* inferential techniques. The capacity to see that a given argument is dubious, in spite of a valid entailment, calls for reflection on the principles of inference involved. A quick glance at a proof of the theorem in question will indicate how much logic is involved in such reflection and how far it takes us from Plato—indeed, from ancient Greece.

A second objection against the claim that Plato might have thought the argument to be acceptable (in the face of the fact that he saw the contradiction contained in the premises) dismisses all the talk about the sophisticatedness of "$(p \& {-}p) \supset q$" as irrelevant. Not the *reasoning* of the TMA causes the problem, but the simple fact that its premises contain a contradiction. Surely Plato did not think that he could derive a true conclusion from premises of which he knew that at least one *had* to be false. And if Plato did recognize the premises of the TMA as incompatible, he would not have thought the argument to be sound. A reply to this objection will take me to a second consideration regarding the TMA, one that calls for a modification of Vlastos' reading of it.

Vlastos concludes his analysis of the TMA with this assertion of Parmenides: "So another form of Largeness will come into view, over and above Largeness itself and its participants" (132a10–11);[65] he justifies his ending at this point by noting that "to go on, as Parmenides does in our argument (132a11–b2), to imply that infinitely many more F-nesses may be deduced by iteration of the reasoning, is from the strictly logical point of view a pure bonus."[66] While it is of course entirely

---

65. This is in *iii* of the quotation on p. 155.
66. *Vlastos, 1969b*, p. 292.

correct that " 'If only one, then two' . . . is as fatal to the refutand as is . . . 'if only one, then infinitely many,' "[67] Vlastos may be missing an important feature of the argument by not going on to its end.

"And again," Parmenides continues, "covering all these yet another, which will make all of them large," (132b1) after which he concludes triumphantly: "So each of your forms will no longer be one, but an indefinite number" (132b1–2).[68] The one form[69] has become many. Now clearly, the "no longer" (*ouketi*) here is not temporal; it does not indicate passage of time: Parmenides does not think that the form has *become* many by some process of fission. Instead, he is saying, "the one form *is* many, Socrates, but you notice it only now because before this you were not aware what pointing to a form entails."

This final conclusion of the TMA is not simply false; it does not merely state a proposition that contradicts a certain theory of forms. What it says is impossible; the statement is self-contradictory, absurd. The TMA may well be correctly read as a *reductio* argument.[70]

I shall not defend this last assertion, but instead shall restate the argument without attempting to remain entirely faithful to the text. I do this because I believe a lesson can be learned about Plato's aim with the TMA—if it is considered as an example of a *reductio* argument—even if the formulation is something of an ideal type.

Suppose, then, that the TMA were statable as follows:[71]

---

67. *Ibid.*

68. This is *iv* in the quotation on pp. 155–156.

69. ἓν ἕκαστον, just one: the same expression at the outset of the argument (132a1) as at the end (132b1). See the discussion in *Vlastos, 1969b*, pp. 293–297 and notes.

70. A suggestion to this effect is to be found in Strang, "Plato and the Third Man," pp. 148–149, though it is not there worked out.

71. To facilitate comparison with the earlier formulation, I shall pretend that Parmenides concludes with an equally absurd, "so each of your forms will no longer be one, but two."

Begin with these assumptions:

> *2.1.* If *x* is *F*, there is a unique form *F*-ness, such that *x* is
> *F* by participating in that *F*-ness. (See *1.1.*)
>
> *2.2.* *a, b, c* are *F*. (See *1.2.*)

from which we can conclude that

> *2.3.* There is a unique form *F*-ness.

If we now introduce another assumption, namely *SP*,

> *2.4.* *F*-ness is *F*,

we can derive (from *2.1* and *2.4*) that

> *2.5.* There is a unique form *F*-ness.

With the *NI* assumption,

> *2.6.* If *x* is *F* by participating in *F*-ness, then $x \neq F$-ness,

we can derive (with the aid of *2.3* and *2.5*) that

> *2.7.* *F*-ness in *2.3* $\neq$ *F*-ness in *2.5*,

which, given that *2.1*, yields

> *2.8.* *F*-ness in *2.1* = *F*-ness in *2.3* and *F*-ness in *2.5*, where
> *F*-ness in *2.3* $\neq$ *F*-ness in *2.5*, which is absurd.

If the TMA appeared in this form, it would not, in its *formal* characteristics, differ from uncontroversial *reductio* or indirect proofs. Consider a familiar example, such as this demonstration of a metatheorem in the propositional calculus: To show that

> *3.5.* If '$A \supset B$' is a tautology and '*A*' is a tautology, then
> '*B*' is a tautology,

a proof may be constructed by assuming the theorem's falsity:

> *3.1.* Suppose that '$A \supset B$' and '*A*' are tautologies and that
> '*B*' is not a tautology.

    3.2. If '*B*' is not a tautology, there is an assignment of truth value to '*B*' such that '*B*' is false.

    3.3. By the hypothesis that both '*A⊃B*' and '*A*' are tautologies, '*A⊃B*' is true for that assignment of truth value to '*B*'.

    3.4. But if '*B*' is false, then, since '*A*' is true, '*A⊃B*' is false.

    3.5. Therefore, since *3.3* and *3.4* are contradictories, if '*A⊃B*' and '*A*' are tautologies '*B*' is a tautology.

The method of proof calls for the deducing of a contradiction from the denial of the proposition to be demonstrated; the original proposition is thus shown to be true. As the argument was stated, its aim—that is, just what was to be demonstrated—was made explicit. But suppose now that one wished to hide one's intention from the reader; the argument might then be restated in such a way so as to show that a contradiction follows from certain premises, without indicating just what the argument is meant to establish. Formally speaking, however, the argument would nevertheless be the same.

Begin with these assumptions:

    4.1. '*A⊃B*' is a tautology.

    4.2. '*A*' is a tautology.

    4.3. '*B*' is not a tautology.

Then, from *4.2* and the definition of "tautology," we can derive

    4.4. There is no assignment of truth value to '*A*' such that '*A*' is false,

while that definition and *4.3* yields

    4.5. There is an assignment of truth value to '*B*' such that '*B*' is false.

The definition of "⊃" allows us to say that

    4.6. If '*A*' is true and '*B*' is false, then '*A⊃B*' is false,

so that from *4.4, 4.5,* and *4.6* we deduce

4.7. There is an assignment of truth value to '*A*' and to '*B*' such that '*A* ⊃ *B*' is false.

But *4.2* and the definition of "tautology" yields

4.8. There is no assignment of truth value to '*A*' and '*B*' such that '*A* ⊃ *B*' is false.

If we now conjoin *4.7* and *4.8*, we can write a conclusion that closely parallels that of the restated TMA (*2.8*):

4.9. Therefore, there is and there is not an assignment of truth value to '*A*' and '*B*' such that '*A* ⊃ *B*' is false, which is absurd.

What the argument shows is that from certain premises and by means of certain definitions and rules of inference, one can derive the contradictory statements, *4.7* and *4.8*, or the self-contradictory conjunction, *4.9*. We therefore know that something has to go; but in the absence of further information, we are free to choose among several possibilities—or better, we won't know *which* to pick. We can throw out any of the assumptions and conclude either

4.91. Therefore, since *4.7* and *4.8* are contradictories, if '*A*' is a tautology and '*B*' is not a tautology, '*A* ⊃ *B*' is not a tautology.

or

4.92. Therefore, since *4.7* and *4.8* are contradictories, if '*A* ⊃ *B*' is a tautology and '*B*' is not a tautology, '*A*' is not a tautology;

or

4.93. Therefore, since *4.7* and *4.8* are contradictories, if '*A* ⊃ *B*' and '*A*' are tautologies, '*B*' is a tautology (i.e., the theorem).

The TMA seen as a *reductio* argument (*2.1–2.8*) is quite like the argument that begins with *4.1* and has *4.9* as its conclusion.

And if we thought that it actually expressed Plato's intention, we should not at all be inclined to judge the argument to be flawed. Just as the self-contradictory statement *4.9* is derived from three premises (*4.1, 4.2, 4.3*) that are incompatible (though this is by no means obvious to everyone!), so the absurd conclusion that one form is two (*2.8*) is deduced from premises about forms and particulars that are incompatible as well.

Nor should we be surprised that Plato did not formulate the TMA in the fashion of a textbook *reductio,* such as *3.1–3.5,* for example, even if we assumed that he was fully clear about the indirect method of proof. Plato is not fond of presenting the reader with a finished piece of doctrine; his entire career testifies to the fact that he is intent on having him think things through for himself. Thus the TMA (still assuming that Plato intended the conclusion as *2.8* formulates it) would be a powerful argument directed against at least one of the premises from which the self-contradiction follows, and the argument would have to be regarded as silent as to *which* of its premises was to be eliminated and why.

How much of this view of the TMA would one be justified in holding? Two significant steps may, I think, be taken in its direction. First, Plato surely did not take the conclusion of the TMA to be false in just the sense in which "Socrates is straight-nosed" is false. The latter *happens* to be false, though it *might* have been true. Plato, however, would surely not have conceded that "each of your forms will no longer be one, but an indefinite number" (132b1–2) just *might* have been true. We may take Plato to have regarded the conclusion of the TMA as wrongheaded in some fundamental way, even if we don't think that he saw it as self-contradictory and if we do not attribute to him some theory of types of falsity.

Second, we may observe that Plato's Socrates had long been in the habit of taking another man's assumptions and, together with other premises, deriving totally hopeless conclusions from them. Even supposing that Plato did not have a clear

understanding of the nature of *reductio* proofs, we may nevertheless attribute to him adherence to the informal dictum, "a
messy conclusion from messy premises comes." Socrates frequently exploits this principle, but two examples must suffice
here. Cratylus maintains that *A* represents *B* only if it does so
perfectly. From this (and other premises) Socrates derives the
conclusion that a perfect representation of Cratylus is not a
representation at all, but another Cratylus.[72] Polemarchus
defines justice as helping friends and harming enemies.
Socrates, by a somewhat longer route, concludes from this that
it is a part of justice to make someone unjust.[73] In both cases,
conclusions that are in some way absurd—and not just false—
are drawn from odd premises. The TMA is not so different.

This entire discussion seems to me to warrant the conclusion
that Plato was not worried about the propriety of the inference of the TMA and not perplexed by the argument with
which he had Parmenides drive Socrates against the wall.
Rather, he took himself to be showing successfully that at least
one of the premises on which the argument rests must be rejected. The TMA does not by itself tell us which premise is to
be given up; we must continue on in the dialogue to see Plato's
position unfold. I shall therefore simply conclude this section
by remarking briefly on what I take to be the fate of the three
operative premises.

First, "If *a*, *b*, and *c*, etc., are *F*, there exists a unique
form, *F*-ness, etc." (*1.1*). Plato does not give up the forms and
hence not this thesis. Socrates continues to assert it in the dialogue, and Parmenides encourages him.[74] In subsequent dialogues Plato continues to maintain a theory of forms.[75]

Second, "If *x* is *F* by participating in *F*-ness, then $x \neq$
F-ness" (*NI*). Plato continues to maintain a non-identity as-

72. *Cratylus* 432a–c; see Ch. 1, pp. 24–25, above.
73. *Republic* 332d–336a.
74. See Secs. VI–VIII.
75. See Secs. VIII and IX.

sumption, though it does not necessarily take this form. Much of the rest of *Parmenides*, Part I, seeks to clarify just in what way there is a gap between particulars and forms.[76]

Third, "*F*-ness is *F*" (*SP*). This is the assumption about forms aimed at by the TMA; it must go. It is at the heart of the metaphysical conception of the forms and disastrous for the logical view.[77] That the TMA seeks to reject this premise can, however, find positive corroboration. After a brief interlude in which Socrates speculates that the forms might be thoughts, Parmenides produces a second version of the TMA and there aims much more explicitly at the self-predication assumption. Before turning, therefore, to Socrates' flirtation with conceptualism, I shall discuss the second version of the Third Man Argument.

VI. Participation: Third Man Argument, Second Version (132d–133a)

Socrates suggests that the forms are "patterns fixed in the nature of things" and that "the other things are made in their image and are likenesses" (132d1–3). By means of a few lines, Parmenides derives a regress from Socrates' fresh position. "A second form will always make its appearance over and above the first form, and if that second form is like anything, yet a third . . ." (132e7–133a1). The structure of this argument of Parmenides' may be exhibited in a way analogous to that of the first version of the TMA:

> *5.1.* If *A*, *b*, and *c*, etc., are similar in respect to being *F*, then there exists a unique form, *F*-ness, such that *a*, *b*, and *c*, etc., participate in *F*-ness by way of the resem-

---

76. See Secs. VI–VIII.

77. This is the strongest version of my thesis. It may also be that Plato merely distinguishes two conceptions of forms without ever relinquishing either of them. See Sec. IX.

blance copies have to the model in the image of which they are made.

5.2 a, b, and *c* are *F.*

SP. F-ness is *F.*

5.3. a, b, c, and *F*-ness are *F.*

NI. If *x* is *F* by participating in *F*-ness, then *x* ≠ *F*-ness.

5.4. Therefore, there exists a unique form, *F*-ness *II,* such that *a, b, c,* and *F*-ness participate in *F*-ness *II* by way of the resemblance copies have to the model in the image of which they are made.

Formally, the two versions of the TMA are the same: both of them show that not all the premises from which the undesirable conclusion is drawn can be maintained. But here the doubt as to which of the premises is to be discarded is resolved. In the second version of the TMA, Parmenides goes to considerable length to bring out the importance of self-predication.

First he asks whether "if a thing is made in the image of the form, can that form fail to be like the image of it, in so far as the image was made in its likeness?" (132d5–7). He then continues by asserting a general principle of which the case under discussion is an instance: "If a thing is like, must it not be like something that is like it?" (132d8). When Socrates assents to this, Parmenides hammers in the point still further: "And must not the thing which is like, share with the thing that is like it in one and the same thing or character?" (132d9–e1).[78] Then back to the particular case, "And will not that in which the like things share, so as to be alike, be just the form itself that you spoke of?" (132e3–4).[79] Plato has Parmenides take great

---

78. Or, very literally, "The like to the like (τὸ δὲ ὅμοιον τῷ ὁμοίῳ), is there not a great necessity for both of them to share in the one same thing?" To be sure, Burnet brackets the εἴδους at 132e1; but clearly nothing else could be meant.

79. More literally, "Whatever it is by virtue of their participation in which like things are like, will not that thing be the form itself?"

pains to show Socrates that the likeness that holds between particulars and forms is symmetrical—even if he lacks the technical language with which to express such a fact most economically. And he makes it utterly clear, as well, that the forms must have the same characteristic as the "thing that has been rendered like to it (*eikasthênai*)" (132d3–4).

Moreover, Parmenides makes it plain that he takes the unpleasant conclusion of the argument to depend precisely on the self-predication assumption. "It is not possible," Parmenides drives home his point, "for anything to be like the form nor the form to be like anything else, otherwise, above and beyond the form there will always be revealed another form and, if it is like anything, another form in turn" (132e6–133a3).[80]

The critique of the self-predication assumption here no longer depends on forms thought of as physical objects. The crude and limited analogy of the sail has been replaced by the very abstract consideration of the symmetricalness of the relation between form and particulars. This attack on the assumption of self-predication—and with it, on the conception of forms as exemplars—is thus much more powerful than the earlier one. Yet just because this version of the TMA does not suppose that forms and particulars are of the same type, some commentators have been led to maintain that it is not directed against a conception of forms as paradigms. For it is held that such a doctrine does not require self-predication.

One attempt to deny the symmetricalness of the relation between pattern-forms and copy-particulars has been frequently refuted. A. E. Taylor has rightly observed that the relation between original and copy is not symmetrical: the model cannot be said to be a copy of the portrait.[81] But the relationship is complex: one component, the derivation of the copy from the original, is indeed asymmetrical, whereas the resemblance of

---

80. Using a very literal translation. Parmenides could hardly have tied the conclusion more closely to the self-predication assumption without saying so in so many words.

81. A. E. Taylor, *Plato: The Man and His Work*, p. 358.

the one to the other is not.[82] And this resemblance, so much stressed in the second version of the TMA, is all that is needed for the present analysis of the argument.

A more sophisticated argument bases its claim that the pattern-copy relationship does not imply self-predication on the fact that forms and particulars are not entities of the same sort.[83] Because forms are eternal and unchanging, while particulars are temporal and in flux, because forms are perfect "causes," while particulars are imperfect effects, they occupy radically different worlds. From this the consequence is drawn that nothing that is said of an entity of the one type can be univocally asserted about one of the other types. A predicate, when applied to a form, *means* something different from what it does when it is applied to a particular. There is no characteristic which is the same in both form and particular; there is no symmetrical relation of resemblance.

Two examples are meant to make the relationship more intelligible. The standard yard which serves as the ultimate measure of all yardsticks we buy and use cannot be said to be one yard long in the way in which we correctly say this of a yardstick we have just bought. Presumably, to assert of our own yardstick that it is one yard long is to say that if it were placed next to the standard yard, it would be seen to have the same length as that paradigm. But, because the paradigm *is* the standard, we cannot compare it, in turn, with anything else. Hence the predicate, "is a yard long," when applied to it, has a different meaning from what it has when attributed to my yardstick. A scarf, to take a second example from R. E.

---

82. References to the various refutations of Taylor's error can be found in *Vlastos, 1954,* p. 242.

83. R. E. Allen, "Participation and Predication in Plato's Middle Dialogues," *Philosophical Review,* 69 (1960), reprinted in Allen, *Studies in Plato's Metaphysics.* Page numbers refer to the reprinted version. While my discussion is aimed at Allen's essay, I believe similar arguments apply to A. L. Peck, "Plato *versus* Parmenides," *Philosophical Review,* 71 (1962), and R. S. Bluck, "The *Parmenides* and the 'Third Man.'"

Allen's paper, "can be bought and sold, lost or stolen,"[84] and so on, whereas the reflection of a scarf is a very different sort of thing and cannot be put to any such uses.

> *The very being of a reflection is relational, wholly dependent upon what is other than itself: the original and the reflecting medium. It is for this reason that, though you may call the reflection of a red scarf red if you so please, you cannot mean the* same *thing you mean when you call its original red. The function '. . . is red' is, in this case, systematically ambiguous. It follows that you cannot say that the reflection stands in relation of color resemblance to its original, since this implies the univocal exemplification of a common quality, presupposed by an assertion of resemblance.*[85]

The example of the scarf puzzles me, in itself and as it applies to the problem of the forms. In one reasonable sense, "red" means exactly the same thing when applied to a scarf and when applied to its reflection. I expect to be able to pick out a red scarf from among others, even if I can see all of them only in a mirror; I should have sufficient confidence in this procedure, moreover, to purchase a scarf in a color to my liking, without seeing it except in reflection. Indeed, one could successfully teach the meaning of "red" solely by means of mirror images of red objects. If we were to understand the meaning of "F" as it applies to F-ness and to a, b, c, etc., in a similar way, there seems no reason to think that self-predication has been abandoned.

Although this is a commonsensical use of "meaning," it is probably not that of the view under discussion. This particular position begins by noting that scarf and reflection are objects of different *sorts* and asserts that *therefore* the meaning of the predicate "red" differs, according to the sort of entity to which it is applied.

Forms (to go to the topic of our real concern) are different

---

84. R. E. Allen, "Participation," p. 50.
85. *Ibid.*

ontological types from particulars; that is, forms and particulars *are* in different ways: "being" is systematically ambiguous with respect to them. *Therefore*, the *F* that holds of *F*-ness is not the same characteristic as that which is true of *a, b,* or *c;* any predicate "*F*" is systematically ambiguous in a way that is analogous to the ambiguity of "being." Two interpretations of this statement are possible, but neither of them, I fear, is very helpful here.

One might maintain that (*a*) the ontological difference or the systematic ambiguity of "being" explains, accounts, or is responsible for a difference in the characters possessed by the different types of entities or for the ambiguity of the predicates. Here some independent sense must be given to "lack of univocal exemplification of a common quality" and to "systematic ambiguity of 'red' or 'just.' "

A second interpretation simply maintains that (*b*) nothing further is meant by this absence of a common character or this ambiguity of predicates other than that the character(s) belong(s) to two types of entities and that the different predicates are attributed to things with respect to which "being" is systematically ambiguous.

I have worries when I consider these views simply *an sich* and when I try to think of them as Plato's. Regarding interpretation (*a*), I should wish to know in what way the characteristics possessed are different (because the possessor is different) and just how "just," say, differs in meaning, depending on whether Justice is just or Socrates is. I should further like to know what it is about the ontological difference that (in some appropriate sense of the term) brings about the difference in character or predicate. Finally, I should be very curious to discover where in Plato these questions are broached, not to mention answered. As the tone of these questions suggests, I find no answers to them in Allen's paper and am very doubtful that they can be answered at all.

Interpretation (*a*), however, is probably not what was intended, so that there may be no point to the questions I raise regarding it. Yet the position given in interpretation (*b*) is no more felicitous. Nothing prevents us from saying that " 'F' is systematically ambiguous" precisely in that " 'F' is attributed to entities of different types," and that, in the same sense, there are different qualities F_1 and F_2 that characterize forms and particulars respectively. While we thus get a distinction, what *difference* does it take account of? Perhaps I am blind to a significant point in metaphysics, but I cannot help thinking that this alleged difference in meaning or this failure to have univocal exemplification of a common quality merely registers a verbal point. By means of it, a self-prediction assumption is precluded and the TMA cannot get started; but the means are frivolous and do not touch on the real issues regarding the relation between forms and particulars.

Finally, there seems to be no basis for the claim that Plato held this position. Even if we suppose him to have taken "being" to be systematically ambiguous—surely an anachronistic way of discussing the degrees of reality view conveyed by the Divided Line—there seems to be no evidence at all that the meaning of "just" changes when something is just eternally, rather than merely for a time; or if it is just purely, rather than conjoined with other traits, etc. Moreover, to attribute to Plato the position now under discussion requires us to accuse him of exploiting the power of the metaphors to copy, resemble, reflect, etc., while rejecting the very features of these metaphors which give them that power and, with it, their attractiveness as models for the way in which forms and particulars are related. Before venturing such a critique, one would wish to find a good basis in the texts.

The relationship between the standard yard and an ordinary yardstick, to move very briefly to the other analogy, raises a number of interesting general problems. Several times, recently, it has also been taken up in connection with the TMA.[86] Right here, however, I wish to confine my comments

---

86. Besides, R. E. Allen, "Participation," see especially P. T. Geach, "The Third Man Again," *Philosophical Review*, 65 (1956), reprinted in

to a single point. The standard *is* different from the yardstick which is manufactured according to it: the ordinary yardstick can and the standard yard cannot be *measured* by the standard yard. Nevertheless, there *must* be a sense, to paraphrase P. T. Geach, in which the standard yard must be a yard;[87] for how could it otherwise be the standard against which the ordinary yard is measured? In the end, it must be possible to say of a well-crafted yardstick that it has the same length as the standard yard.[88] In short, if there is a difference in the meaning of "is a yard long" when applied to the standard and to the ordinary stick, there must also be overlap. "Like" does not need to mean "like in all respects"; it is enough for the TMA and for self-predication that "like" holds in *some* respects, that some symmetricalness is preserved.

One final note. Suppose for the sake of argument that sense could be made of an asymmetrical resemblance that allowed copies to be made of originals without self-predication; why should we think that Plato held such a view? One place where Plato reflects fairly self-consciously on the nature of representing or copying is in connection with the argument of the two Cratyluses already referred to.[89] Socrates there points out that in order for there to be a perfect representation of Cratylus, that representation would have to be another Cratylus, indistinguishable from the first. To whatever degree one thing is like another—this is the assumption underlying this argument —to that degree the two things share the same characteristic. Were this not so, the appearance of a second Cratylus need not be feared. There is no reason to suppose that here in the *Parmenides* Plato is withdrawing an assumption which is not

---

Allen, *Studies in Plato's Metaphysics,* as well as Strang, "Plato and the Third Man." The latter two acknowledge a debt to Wittgenstein.

87. P. T. Geach, "The Third Man Again," p. 276.

88. See Gregory Vlastos, "Postscript to the Third Man: A Reply to Mr. Geach," *Philosophical Review,* 65 (1956), reprinted in Allen, *Studies in Plato's Metaphysics,* especially pp. 284–286.

89. See pp. 24–25 and 169, above.

only commonsensical but, in the *Cratylus,* served Plato as a
premise of an excellent argument seriously intended.[90]

In the second version of the Third Man Argument, Plato
elaborates and drives home the conclusion he had intended
even in its original appearance. He first leads one to a conclusion that is clearly unacceptable, thus forcing one to reexam-
ine the premises on which it depended. The second version of
the TMA then makes it fully clear that it is the assumption of
self-predication that must be rejected.

VII. FORMS AS THOUGHTS (132b-c)

The first version of the Third Man Argument left open which
of its premises should be rejected; the second version settles
the ambiguity. Sandwiched between these two ways of presenting the TMA is an argument that deals with this issue in
a somewhat different way: it indicates that the "separation"
of forms from particulars is *not* to be dispensed with. Indeed,
all the rest of this first part of the *Parmenides* is devoted to
"separation": the present argument insists that forms must be
separate from and not assimilated to particulars, while the
final argument (133b–134e) warns against carrying this separation to excess.

In an attempt to escape the consequences of the TMA, Socrates embraces the desperate hypothesis "that each of these
forms is a thought, which cannot properly exist anywhere but
in a mind" (132b3–5). He hopes that in this way many particulars can participate in a single form without having the form
itself multiply.

For a moment it looks as if Socrates were proposing a con-
ceptualist solution, but no attempt whatever is made to work

---

90. Nor are there any linguistic shifts as one goes from the two
Cratyluses argument to the TMA. In both cases, the key terms are
εἰκών and ὅμοιον and words compounded of them.

it out. Parmenides, in his first objection to the new hypothesis, ignores altogether the fact that thoughts have been brought into the picture. Instead, he reminds Socrates that his problem —the problem of participation—is brought on by the one-many relation and focuses simply on the *one-ness* of the newly introduced thoughts. Quickly Socrates is led to admit that what he proposes must be a thought "of some *one* thing which that thought observes to cover all the cases, as being a certain single character" (132c3–4); and to this the TMA applies.

Socrates might as well not have been talking about thoughts, but of the objects of thoughts that are not themselves thoughts. Socrates gives in without a murmur and makes no effort to insist on a distinction between thoughts and their objects. So far, one can hardly speak of the introduction of a conceptualism.

The second part of Parmenides' objection does take seriously that "each of these forms is a thought" (132b8–9); still, there is no exploration of this thesis. Immediately, Parmenides drives to the conclusion, first that "each of those things [that have a share in the forms] consists of thoughts," and if that is so, that either "all things think, or else that they are thoughts which nevertheless do not think" (132c9–11). This later disjunction is flamboyant embroidery designed to point up how absurd it would be to suppose that the world is composed of thoughts. The crucial step here is the first, that particulars should themselves be thoughts. I shall first summarize the argument and then comment on each step.

From two premises that are asserted,

6.1. a, b, and *c* are *F* by participating in *F*-ness,
6.2. F-ness is a thought,

together with a premise that is not made explicit,

6.3. If *x* is *F* by participating in *F*-ness, then *x* is of the same ontological type as *F*-ness,

the conclusion is derived that

6.4. a, b, and *c* are thoughts.

The first premise *(6.1)* is not new, but has been assumed all along. Plato, moreover, goes to some length to remind the reader of the continuity of this argument with what has preceded. Socrates begins with "may it not be that each of these forms . . ." (132b3–4), thus referring to the forms discussed in the TMA. And Parmenides emphasizes this continuity by starting off his second objection with "according to the way in which you assert that the other things have a share in the forms . . ." (132c9–10), in this way harking back to Socrates' earlier introduction of participation. The second premise *(6.2)* simply states explicitly the hypothesis under discusion, that "each of these forms is a thought" (132b8–9).

But *6.1* and *6.2* are not enough to yield the conclusion Parmenides reaches *(6.4)*. An additional premise is needed, one which asserts that whatever shares in a form is the same sort of thing as the form. Without such an assumption—call it the ontological identity assumption *(OI)*—a form might well be a thought, while particulars remain physical objects. Any understanding of Plato's view of *OI,* however, presupposes some further reflections on the conclusion of the argument *(6.4)*.

There is every reason to believe that Plato never took seriously the doctrine that forms should be thoughts. Not only does it get very little play in the present passage, but it is also worth noting that this doctrine is sharply antithetical to views he expresses elsewhere. The objectivist streak is a strong one in all of Plato's work. The Divided Line distinguishes between states of mind and objects of those states: knowledge is of objects that are there, independent of the activity of any mind. When, in the *Timaeus,* Plato has the opportunity to convert the forms into thoughts of a divinity, he emphatically does not take it. The forms are there for the demiurge to apprehend.[91] Not even god is the measure of all things, let alone man.

---

91. *Timaeus* 51b–52a. But see Kevin F. Doherty, S. J., Location of the Platonic Ideas," *The Review of Metaphysics,* 14 (1960), 57–72.

Accordingly, Plato in no sense expects the reader to be attracted to the thesis that forms are thoughts; the point of the argument is to exhibit the unacceptability of what I have dubbed the ontological identity assumption. *OI* is dangerous. Not only can it be used to infer that the familiar world consists either of unthought or of unthinking thoughts, but, by means of it, havoc can be worked in several additional ways. Given

> *6.1. a, b,* and *c* are *F* by participating in *F*-ness

and the controversial premise

> *OI.* If *x* is *F* by participating in *F*-ness, then *x* is of the same ontological type as *F*-ness,

then, with various perfectly reasonable premises about particulars, we can derive devastating conclusions about forms. Thus with

> *6.5. a, b,* and *c* are physical objects,

we can deduce

> *6.6. F*-ness is a physical object;

with the aid of

> *6.7. a, b,* and *c* are human acts,

we get

> *6.8. F*-ness is a human act;

and

> *6.9. a, b,* and *c* are temporal entities

yields

> *6.10. F*-ness is a temporal entity.

In short, by means of the ontological identity assumption we can wipe out all the differences between particulars and forms that are important for Plato. Particulars are changing and unstable, whereas forms are changing and stable; particulars are objects of perception, whereas forms are objects of intellection; particulars are merely objects of belief, whereas only forms are knowable. *OI* is so ruinous because it serves to assimilate the forms into the world of observation. Such emasculated forms retain no properties by virtue of which they *are* forms, so that they can perform none of the functions which was at any time assigned to them. Above all, if the forms are to secure the significance of all discourse by constituting something on which one can fix one's thoughts, they must be clearly distinguishable from any and all particulars to be found in the world of sense.

One might have thought that once self-predication was abandoned, the non-identity thesis could be given up as well. For if *F*-ness is *not F,* then, since *a, b,* and *c are F,* particular and form cannot in any case be identical and *NI* would be gratuitous. Our present argument, however, warns us that *NI* must in effect be strengthened in order to rule out, among other possibilities, that both particular and form be (non-identical) physical objects. Without some "separation" assumption, the Platinum Standard Yard kept somewhere in Washington could quite literally be the form of the yardstick I own. Form and particular, in the language of the Divided Line, must not be located on the same level of existence. A denial of *OI* is called for; indeed, we may assert an Ontological Non-Identity assumption.

> *ONI.* If *x* is *F* by participating in *F*-ness, then *x* is not of the same ontological type as *F*-ness.

By drawing conclusions from *OI* that are totally unacceptable, Plato exhibits the need for this separation.

VIII. Separation: (1) Forms as Unknowables (133b–134c)

Parmenides introduces the final problem he will pose regarding the theory of forms by saying that it is "the worst difficulty" (133b4), though he does not think it to be insuperable. "A man of wide experience and natural ability," one who was "willing to follow one through a long and remote train of argument," (133b7–9) could succeed in showing that the objection about to be made can be overcome. When Socrates' natural ability comes to be informed by dialectic, he will also become clearer about the objects of the method. As this part of the dialogue ends, bridges are being built to the second portion and to later works.

The "worst difficulty" is an argument proposing to show that the forms, "if they are such as we are saying they must be, cannot even be known" (133b5–7). The argument, much wordier than any of the others, contains ambiguities and is not easy to state clearly—characteristics that are surely related to the fact that the argument is not sound and is known by Plato to be faulty. I shall state a somewhat streamlined version of it:[92]

> 7.1. *F*-ness, *G*-ness, etc., do not exist in the world of *a*, *b*, etc., which are *F* and *G*, etc.[93]
> 7.2. *F*-ness, *G*-ness, etc., have their being by virtue of standing in relation to each other and not by standing in relation to *a*, *b*, etc., which are *F*, *G*, etc.[94]

---

92. The text upon which the argument is based will be given in footnotes, while each step will be commented upon immediately below.

93. "You or anyone else who asserts that each of them [the forms] has real being 'just by itself,' would admit . . . that no such real being exists in our world (ἐν ἡμῖν i.e., *chez nous*)" (133c3–5).

94. "Those forms which are what they are with reference to one another (πρὸς ἀλλήλας) have their being in such references among them-

7.3. *a, b,* etc., which are *F, G,* etc., stand in relation to
each other and not to *F*-ness, *G*-ness, etc.[95]

7.4. Knowledge itself is knowledge of *F*-ness, *G*-ness,
etc.[96]

7.5. Any particular man who has knowledge knows only
a, b, etc.[97]

But since *7.1* and *7.4,*

7.6. No particular man who has knowledge knows *F*-ness,
G-ness, etc.[98]

No knowledge, that is, which men can possess can be knowledge of the forms.

The first premise (*7.1*) declares the forms to be separate
from the world of becoming. The unknowability of the forms

---

selves (πρὸς αὐτὰς), not with reference (πρὸς) to those likenesses or whatever we are to call them, in our world, which we possess and so come to be called by their several names" (133c8–d2).

95. "These things in our world which bear the same names as the forms are related among themselves (πρὸς αὐτά), not to the forms" (133d2–4).

96. "And similarly Knowledge itself, the essence of Knowledge, will be Knowledge of that Reality itself, the essentially Real (Οὐκοῦν καὶ ἐπιστήμη αὐτὴ . . . ὃ ἔστιν ἐπιστήμη τῆς ὃ ἔστιν ἀλήθεια αὐτῆς ἂν ἐκείνης εἴη ἐπιστήμη)" (134a3–4). This is unusually emphatic in its stress on absolute Knowledge and its knowledge of absolute Truth. The separateness of both these from ordinary knowledge of ordinary things is pointed up. Parmenides here even goes to the trouble to make the point again for "any given branch of knowledge" (134a10).

I have left out the example by means of which Parmenides works up to the case of knowledge: Mastership is related only to Slavery, while a master is related only to his slave.

97. "The knowledge in our world will be knowledge of the reality in our world, and it will follow again that each branch of knowledge in our world must be knowledge of some department of things that exist, in our world" (134a9–b1). This is followed by "necessarily" (ἀνάγκη), which accounts for the "only" in this step.

98. "We do not possess the forms themselves, nor can they exist in our world. . . . And presumably the forms, just as they are in themselves, are known by the form of Knowledge itself? . . . the form which we do not possess. . . . Then, none of the forms is known by us, since we have no part in knowledge itself" (134b3–12).

is derived from it in the sense that the other steps in the argument are seen as consequences or applications of this fact of separation. The argument is an exploration of the doctrine of separation and a warning against a possible interpretation of it.

The negative side of the second premise (7.2), that forms do not obtain their being by virtue of standing in relation to particulars, is precisely what has been meant all along by the absolute[99] and independent character of the forms. The positive clause, however, introduces a new element into the discussion. That the forms should obtain their being from the relations they have to each other suggests not only the set of exploratory arguments of the second part of the *Parmenides,* but also looks forward to the kind of dialectic that is announced and discussed in the *Phaedrus* and exemplified in the *Statesman* and the *Sophist.* By itself, this premise is but the product of a doctrine of separation and the assumption that there is at least some order in the realm of forms. The next premise, however, forces an interpretation on this doctrine of separation which leads to the unhappy consequences of Parmenides' argument.

The affirmative clause of the next step (7.3) is sensible and innocent enough: particulars are related to particulars. thus constituting our familiar world. The doctrine of separation, moreover, requires that particulars not be related to forms in the same way in which they are related to each other. Forms and particulars must not interact in the manner in which particulars interact with each other. Parmenides gives an example: a person who is a master will be master over a slave, another person, and not over Slavery itself, the form. But the second and negative portion of this premise takes the separation much further than that: it rules out any relation whatsoever between particulars and forms. No room is left for a distinction between types of relations. The interaction that takes place between a particular master and a particular slave is made to stand for

---

99. E.g., αὐτὸ τὸ ὅ ἐστιν (*Phaedo* 74d6).

all possible relations. And since *such* relations are impossible between particulars and forms, it is taken for granted that there can be no relations at all. Thus *no* meaning can be given to "participation," for there can be no such thing.

In effect, we are talking about three types of relations: R_1, relations holding among particulars; R_2, relations that hold among forms; and R_3, relations that obtain between particulars and forms. A gratuitous by-product of Parmenides' insistence on the reality of the types of relations R_1 and R_2 is the claim that there are no relations at all of type R_3.

The fourth step of the argument (7.4) asserts that the form of knowledge knows the forms and thus expresses a confusion between relations of type R_1 and R_2. Parmenides' saying that the forms have their being by virtue of the relations they have vis à vis one another, implies that finding out what being a form actually is requires one to engage in the sort of investigations carried on in the *Statesman* and *Sophist*. But now the talk is of the Mastership over Slavery itself and of the form of Knowledge knowing forms: it seems as if an inquiry into the relations that hold among forms is like empirical research into the goings-on among particulars, where one tries to find out who does what to whom. To suppose that the form of Knowledge knows anything at all is to take the forms to be related to one another precisely in the way particulars are.

Self-predication, here, is a by-product of this confusion between types of relations, but it works in a peculiar way. The form of Knowledge cannot know everything, but only forms; the form of Mastery does not command the services of a genuine slave. Here self-predication operates within a framework of sharp separation, within a position in which relations of type R_3—those between forms and particulars—are not admitted.

The final premise (7.5) is an application of what one might call the Axiom of Exaggerated Separateness to the question of knowledge. It says that knowers of this world can know only things of this world. And because we are, presumably, knowers of the world of flux and appearance, we cannot come to know forms.[100]

Parmenides concludes that we cannot know the forms. But in a way, the road by means of which he reaches this goal is even worse than the outcome itself. For the exaggerated interpretation (7.3) of the principle of separation (7.2) rules out any relation between our world and the world of forms, including that of exemplification of the form in the particular. In short, the separation is such that the forms can no longer perform any of the functions which were at one or another time assigned to them.

IX. SEPARATION: (2) GOD'S IGNORANCE OF THE HUMAN WORLD (134c-e)

According to the final argument in this first part of the *Parmenides,* not only would a god not be a master over us or anything in our world, but he could have no knowledge of us or of "anything of human concern" (134e5–6). This consequence "is still more formidable" (134c4), for it makes plainly absurd the claim that god has the most perfect knowledge (134c).

The argument itself is very similar to that which condemns human beings to ignorance of the forms.

> *8.1.* Knowledge itself is more perfect than the knowledge of any man.[101]

---

100. This argument does not accord a special status to the psyche; the soul cannot here be thought of as having the power to range from the lowest to the highest section of the Divided Line. It cannot liberate itself from the cave. Parmenides' argument is not compatible with the view that Plato holds in such dialogues as the *Republic* and the *Phaedrus.*

101. "If there is such a thing as a form, Knowledge itself, it is much more perfect than the knowledge in our world, and so with Beauty and all the rest" (134c6–8). I eliminate the conditional which goes throughout the argument and assume that there *is* a form, etc.

8.2. God has Knowledge itself.[102]

8.3. F-ness, G-ness, etc., have their being by virtue of standing in relation to each other and not by standing in relation to a, b, etc., which are F, G, etc. Same as 7.2)

8.4. a, b, etc., which are F, G, etc., stand in relation to each other and not to F-ness, G-ness, etc. (Same as 7.3)[103]

8.5. Perfect knowledge is only of things in the world of F-ness, G-ness, etc.

8.6. Therefore, god cannot know things in the world of a, b, etc.[104]

No step-by-step commentary is needed, for this argument is not significantly different from the previous one. It rests again on a principle of separation that has been pushed so far as to preclude all relations between forms and particulars. This time, instead of looking up from below—or trying to—we are looking down from on high, yet never reaching bottom.

One peculiarity is worth noting. In the previous argument, only the form of Knowledge knows perfectly: no man can have knowledge in a way that would be sufficient for him to know forms. Now, however, something other than Knowledge

---

102. "And if anything has part in this Knowledge itself, you would agree that a god has a better title than anyone else to possess the most perfect Knowledge . . . Knowledge itself . . . ?" (134c10–d2). The formulation of 8.2 is odd but, I think, accurate. More on this in a moment.

103. "We have agreed that those forms have no significance with reference to things in our world, nor have things in our world any significance with reference to them. Each set has it only among themselves" (134d4–7). Specifically, "we have agreed" at 133c–e, from which 7.2 and 7.3 were originally derived.

104. "Then if this most perfect Mastership and most perfect Knowledge are in the god's world, the gods' Mastership can never be exercised over us, nor their Knowledge know us or anything in our world. . . . They, . . . being gods, are not our masters nor do they know anything of human concerns" (134d9–e6). I have again left out the master-slave example from the formulation.

itself can also know perfectly, a state of affairs that requires
us to make the strange statement (*8.2*) that god has Knowledge
itself. As Cornford puts it, this is a "confusion of the form,
Knowledge, with the perfect instance of knowing."[105] And he
is surely right when he says that "it is in fact the god, not the
form, Knowledge, that knows the forms."[106]

Self-predication adds to the miseries of this argument, but
even if it were eliminated, there would still be trouble. Either
god's knowing is so perfect as to inherit from the form (which
is perfectly exemplified in god) its unrelatedness to the world
of "human concerns," or it is merely an *exemplification* of the
form (however perfect), so that it belongs to the familiar
world—a vantage point from which knowledge of the forms
was seen to be impossible. The difficulty in this final argument
is the excessive separation of particulars and forms. It effectively warns against it.

X. Conclusion

The *Parmenides* is not a dramatic work on the order of the
Protagoras, with its fully drawn characters, its movement, and
its scenery. Nevertheless, the *arguments* of this dialogue, no
less than those of the earlier work, are related to each other in
a dramatic way, for only if one considers them as building
upon each other is it possible to see how Plato uses the interchange between Parmenides and Socrates to revise his theory
of forms. Yet precisely because the effect of this dialogue is
cumulative, a detailed consideration of its various pieces may
have made it difficult to see the forest for the trees, so that it
becomes necessary to summarize the conclusions that have
been reached. Moreover, because the *Parmenides* is properly
understood as a turning point in Plato's reflections about the

---

105. Cornford, *Plato and Parmenides,* p. 98.
106. *Ibid.,* p. 99.

objects and method of knowledge, it will be helpful to give at least a general indication of what the dialogue foreshadows. This I shall now do by singling out three propositions for consideration and by briefly discussing each in turn.

First, there *are* forms of trivial and worthless, as well as of valuable and important, things. Forms are not valuable above all else in the way in which virtue is more valuable than vice; they are of value precisely because they are the ground of intelligibility and the highest objects of knowledge. Second, it is not the case that forms actually *are* the characteristic that is named by their names. Forms are not exemplars; the self-predication assumption does not hold. Third, while forms *are* distinct and different from the particulars of the phenomenal world, they are not so separate as to be unknowable.

(*1*) THE RANGE OF THE REALM OF FORMS. In two later dialogues, the Stranger reminds us in unequivocal terms of the early lesson Parmenides gives to young Socrates. The endeavor of dialectic, he says,

> is to know what is and is not kindred in all arts, with a view to the acquisition of intelligence, and having this in view, he honors them all alike. And when she makes comparisons, she counts one of them not a whit more ridiculous than another, nor does she esteem him who adduces as his example of hunting, the general's art, at all more decorous than another who cites that of the vermin destroyer, but only as the greater pretender of the two. . . . The art of dialectic is in no wise particular about fine words.[107]

And still more succinctly, in the *Statesman*, the Stranger later reminds us "that in a philosophical search for a definition . . . , the presence or absence of dignity in the object under definition is an irrelevance. Lowly and exalted must receive equal consideration and the argument must proceed by proper

---

107. *Sophist* 227b1–c2.

stages in its own right to reach the truest conclusion obtainable."[108] The forms make meaningful discourse possible, regardless of the subject matter of that discourse; and they enable us to know, however undignified the putative object of our knowledge. Our aim may very well be to learn about "the existents which are of highest value and chief importance, [and which] are demonstrable only by reason and are not to be apprehended by any other means." Nevertheless and precisely in order to be able to accomplish this end, "we must train ourselves to give and to understand a rational account of every existent thing."[109]

If mud and hair raise a problem for a conception of forms that allows forms only of the valuable, it is aggravated by certain of the negative forms. If there is a single hierarchy of value that has the forms at its apex, there is no place for a form of Ugliness or of Evil. However, not only are there forms of things that are the very opposite of valuable in Plato's later dialogues, but, in the *Sophist*, Plato generalizes the principle of negative forms just as we should expect him to if the forms are meant to underwrite meaningful discourse and knowledge.[110]

(2) SELF-PREDICATION. The issue of negative forms also poses the problem of self-predication in a particularly sharp way. While it is somehow attractive to think of the form of Beauty as beautiful or the form of Justice as just, it is to an equal degree grating to think of the form of Ugliness as ugly or the form of Injustice as unjust. But there is another range of forms for which self-predication poses even more serious difficulties. Take (to use Vlastos' words)

> *forms like Change, Becoming, and Perishing. . . . Clearly none of these could be self-predicational, for if they were, they would*

---

108. *Statesman* 266d7–9.
109. *Statesman* 286a5–7, 286a4–5.
110. *Sophist* 256d–258c. See J. M. E. Moravcsik, "Being and Meaning in the 'Sophist,'" *Acta Philosophica Fennica*, Fasc. XIV (1962), 70–72, for a discussion of negative forms.

> not be changeless, and would thus forfeit being. The same
> could be said of other Forms not mentioned as such by Plato,
> but which his Theory would require him to recognize—Forms
> of the Sensible, Corporeal, Imperfect, indeed of all characters
> contrary to those which define the conditions of Platonic
> being.[111]

Such considerations led Vlastos to conclude that Plato never
became aware of the fact that his account of the forms assumed that they are self-predicational. There is, of course, no
way of knowing the precise moment when Plato became
aware of the price he had to pay if he was to have the forms
serve as paradigms, but by the time he sat down to write the
Parmenides, he knew he had to purge his doctrine of the self-
predication assumption. The difficulties already mentioned are
sufficient reasons for such a retrenchment, but the unacceptability of *SP* is even more obvious when we consider such forms
as that of Noise (listen to it!) and of Visibility (look at it
now!).[112] Accordingly, *SP* simply does not mean what it
says[113] or no such doctrine can sensibly be maintained. Precisely what it is, however, that Plato gives up when *SP* is abandoned needs further spelling out.

The self-predication assumption is a product of a conception
of forms as paradigms, in a world in which reality ranges from
things that are *F* in a shadowy way to forms that are pre-
eminently *F*. Thus, while *SP* simply says that the character
that is named by the name of the form is predicated of the
form itself, that assumption is a good deal stronger than a

---

111. *Vlastos, 1954,* p. 251.
112. Vlastos (in *Vlastos, 1969a*) is aware of the fact that "the real objection to *SP* is semantic—i.e., its assertion in cases where a form could not
fall within the range of significance of the corresponding predicate . . ."
(p. 76, n. 8). One only wonders why he continues to think that Plato
himself would not come to notice some of these grave difficulties.
113. In which case it is doubtful that it means anything at all. See
Sec. VI, above.

generalization on the order of "all of the apples in this barrel are rotten." For *SP* asserts that any form has the character in question *merely by virtue of the fact that it is a form.* No particular form need be examined, in other words, to see whether self-predication holds of it (as we must examine particular apples to see whether or not they are rotten); we know in advance for any case of *F*-ness that it is *F*.

To say that Plato abandons the self-predication assumption is to claim that he gives up the view that a form, by virtue of being a form, has the character to which it corresponds, a revision that is perfectly compatible with *some* forms possessing that character. For such a case, self-predication does not depend upon the form's being a form, but on its being this rather than that particular form—the form of Being, say, which *is,* rather than the form of Largeness, which is not large. In this view, whether self-predication holds for a given form is then discovered through an examination of that form by means of precisely the sort of analysis that is undertaken in the *Sophist.* Thus, while Plato's revised view permits particular forms to be self-predicative, the self-predication assumption itself (SP), which was needed to derive the regress in the TMA, is no longer part of the doctrine.[114]

Once it is recognized that, for metaphysical as well as logical reasons, the rejection of *SP* does not require us to deny that particular forms may be self-predicative, the problem of self-predication in the dialogues that come after the *Parmenides* disappears. Self-predication is indeed to be found in Plato's later work, but it is not the "automatic" self-predication of

---

114. This may be made somewhat clearer with the help of quantifiers. *SP* might then be made to read like this:

For all forms, if the form is *F*-ness, then it is *F,*

so that the denial of *SP* is:

There is a form, such that the form is *F*-ness and not *F,*

rather than

For all forms, if the form is *F*-ness, it is not *F.*

"Justice is just" or "Largeness is large." Instead, self-predication is asserted only of forms where reasons can be given that pertain to the particular forms in question.[115]

(3) SEPARATION. "Only one course is open to the philosopher who values knowledge and the rest above all else. . . . Like a child begging for 'both,' he must declare that reality or the sum of things is both at once—all that is unchangeable and all that is change."[116] This is Plato's mature view; both the world of particulars which we can observe (the world of flux) and the world of forms possess reality.[117] It does not follow, however, that the portion of reality that does change is as fit to be an object of knowledge as that which does not. Neither in the *Sophist* nor anywhere else does Plato retract the principle that the objects of true knowledge must be changeless and stable, for "how can we ever get a permanent grasp on anything that is entirely devoid of permanence?"[118] The last argument of *Parmenides,* Part I, warns against forms that remain inaccessible to living, and therefore changing, intelligence, although separation must nevertheless not be given up.[119] If the forms, like observable particulars, are thought of as changing, they are no longer fit objects of the highest knowledge. But if, when they are thought of as possessing perfect fixity, they are also held to be immanent in the world we see, the reality of change in that world is undermined in Parmenidean fashion.[120]

---

115. See J. M. E. Moravcsik, "The 'Third Man' Argument," *Phronesis,* pp. 50–62, and *Vlastos, 1969a.*

116. *Sophist* 249c10–d4.

117. I remain silent as to whether Plato ever held a view substantially different from this. For a defense of an affirmative answer, see Francis M. Cornford, *Plato's Theory of Knowledge* (Library of Liberal Arts 100 [Indianapolis: Bobbs-Merrill, 1957]), pp. 242–248.

118. *Philebus* 59b4–5.

119. See *Sophist* 249a–b.

120. See W. F. R. Hardie, *A Study in Plato* (Oxford: Clarendon Press, 1936), p. 76.

While forms must be the things we know, they can never also become "just the things we see."[121]

The *Parmenides* prepares the way for a conception of forms that makes them suitable objects of the method of collection and division. In the *Republic,* dialectic issues in a vision of the sun: to know a form, in the context of the allegory of the cave, is to see it with the mind's eye, to become acquainted with it. In Cherniss' phrase, knowledge consists in "direct contact of subject and object."[122] Such a view of what it is to know lends itself to the comparison of forms with physical objects seen in the light of the sun. Each presents itself as complete and separate, if not isolated, from the others. And if knowing a single form is like seeing an object, coming to know many forms may be compared to collecting apples in an orchard. Each act of plucking is distinct from all previous acts and, except for the fact that with the plucking of the first apple, one has, let us hope, been put into a place where more apples may be found, the initial gathering of apples has no influence on subsequent ones. The forms may indeed constitute a realm, and knowledge of forms may actually be a science. But in these middle dialogues, the forms are not presented as clearly related to each other and the method is not explicitly shown to yield an organized body of knowledge.

The second part of the *Parmenides* investigates a number of hypotheses regarding the relation of the One to other forms. When, in the *Phaedrus,* the new method of dialectic is first announced, it is clearly presented as a method that places forms in relation to each other. "The first [procedure] is that in which we bring a dispersed plurality under a single form, seeing it all together."[123] This is collection. Next, in division, we

---

121. *Parmenides* 130d3–4.
122. H. F. Cherniss, "The Philosophical Economy of the Theory of Ideas," in Allen, *Studies in Plato's Metaphysics,* p. 8. This immediacy of knowledge in Plato has of course been noted by many writers.
123. *Phaedrus* 265d3–4.

"divide into forms, following the objective articulation; we are not to attempt to hack off parts like a clumsy butcher."[124] Whenever the method is discussed or, more important, employed,[125] it becomes clear that its task is to order an entire group of forms. Thus, when, in his search for the Sophist, the Stranger first stumbles on to the Philosopher, he enthusiastically describes the science of dialectic:

> *And the man who can do that discerns clearly one form every-where extended throughout many, where each one lies apart, and many forms, different from one another, embraced from without by one form, and again one form connected in a unity through many wholes, and many forms, entirely marked off apart. That means knowing how to distinguish, kind by kind, in what ways the several kinds can or cannot combine.*[126]

Dialectic, now, organizes a domain, whether it is logic or politics, by seeing how its various components stand in relation to each other.[127] And it is worth reminding ourselves that the objects which are revealed by these "sciences" to constitute an orderly system are not particulars of this world, but forms: *forms* combine or fail to do so in one way rather than another.

Self-predicational paradigms are eminently unfit for such exercises: Parmenides was right to undermine this conception. What meaning could be attached to the notion of "weaving together" or "blending"[128] forms if exemplars or super-particulars were to be so combined? If the paradigm of Man and that of Animal were said to blend, would this not mean that besides being human, the form of Man would also have to be animal? But in such a view, the purity of the form would

---

124. *Phaedrus* 265e1–3.
125. Discussed largely in *Sophist* 253d, *Statesman* 262a–263b, *Philebus* 16c–18d, and employed in those same dialogues.
126. *Sophist* 253d5–e2.
127. In the *Cratylus,* Socrates undoubtedly expects his ideal language to exhibit precisely such an organized domain. See Ch. 1, pp. 35–36, above.
128. E.g., *Sophist* 260a, b.

be violated: just how could it be distinguished *as* a form from ordinary particulars?[129] Forms conceived of as paradigms appear to be subject to blending only in the way in which the baker blends flour and eggs; and there blending is transforming. Only if paradigmatic forms were to stay apart in splendid isolation from each other would they remain what they are.

The objects of collection and division, however, blend; they are capable of standing in relation to each other. Such forms cannot be model instances, but are more like criteria which models of that sort must satisfy. They are not super-things to be seen by the mind's eye, but definitional principles to be arrived at by reflection. To understand these forms is to understand the permanent structures of the things we observe in the world of becoming, although few particulars, if any, can be expected to be perfect exemplifications of the form-standards. Nothing in that world is permanent, nor can anything in it be an exemplification of anything but a single form.

In this way the forms associated with collection and division also fulfill the requirements placed upon the paradigms of the middle dialogues, without being subject to the problems of self-predication. Moreover, the forms of Plato's late dialogues are genuinely objects of knowledge: while it would be wrong to say that they are linguistic in nature, they are very like the definitions that tell us what characteristics things have. And when the blending of some set of given forms is understood and they are seen as combined in various ways, what is then grasped resembles the laws of a science that show how structures are related to each other.[130] Finally, the forms continue

---

129. To have forms blend in this way, moreover, would go far toward wiping out the distinction with which Socrates counters Zeno's original defense of Parmenidean monism. *Parmenides* 128a–130a; see p. 144, above.

130. For recent and suggestive discussions of at least similar ways of regarding the forms in the later dialogues, see the two papers by Moravcsik already cited and R. C. Cross, "Logos and Forms in Plato," *Mind*, 63 (1954), reprinted in Allen, *Studies in Plato's Metaphysics*. Also see G. E. M. Anscombe, "The New Theory of Forms," *The Monist*, 50 (1966). The dis-

to fulfill the semantic function that was, from the beginning, assigned to them. They are each the "one thing" to which a name refers and which, in Plato's account, gives that name univocal meaning.

This later view of forms does not settle the problem of participation with which Parmenides taunts the young Socrates in our dialogue. But when that dialogue begins, the problem is peculiarly Plato's, for his view had required that he see how particulars could participate in forms-as-paradigms. However, after Parmenides and Socrates complete their exchange and purge the forms of their character as exemplars, the problem of participation that remains has become that of the entire philosophic tradition in the West.

XI. Coda on the *Timaeus*

The above account of the fate of Plato's theory of forms in the *Parmenides* shows it to be compatible with the role played by the forms in those of the later dialogues in which the method of collection and division is used. Indeed, the kind of excision of the forms' function as paradigms which takes place in the *Parmenides* is necessary if Plato's later dialectic is to be suited to its objects. One work alone, among the later dialogues—the *Timaeus*—raises fundamental problems with the interpretation here proposed.

In the *Timaeus* the forms are important and they are paradigms. When, "in a few words," a distinction is drawn between objects of belief and intelligence, the account is essentially a summary of what is conveyed by the *Republic*'s Divided Line.[131] Moreover, the things of the world of change are introduced by reference to their *likeness* to forms: "Second is

---

tinction made by Strang between a definition as standard (an analytical or A-*logos*) and an object as standard (a paradigmatic-logos) is particularly helpful. See Strang, "Plato and the Third Man," pp. 154–155.

131. *Timaeus* 51c–52a.

that which bears the same name and is like that Form; is sensible; is brought into existence,"[132] etc. The conception of the forms in the *Timaeus* cannot be reconciled with the conception to which the *Parmenides* turns.

There is no easy solution to this problem; coping with it would call for a large-scale investigation of all Plato's later works. Here I merely wish to suggest three possibilities, without attempting to argue in their support. The first and much the simplest alternative is that the *Timaeus* is not a late work after all, but was written before the *Parmenides*. This claim flies in the face of a long-standing tradition which sees the *Timaeus* as one of the last of Plato's compositions.[133] Nevertheless, the tradition *has* been vigorously challenged: G. E. L. Owen marshals stylometric, historical, and philosophical arguments in support of his contention that the *Timaeus* precedes the writing of the *Parmenides*.[134] If this thesis were correct, there would be no problem concerning the *Timaeus*, for the dialogue could then be regarded as the last in which forms are still paradigms and as more properly listed with the *Phaedo* and the *Republic*. One article, however, does not overthrow the tradition, and this particular challenge has evoked an especially powerful defense. H. F. Cherniss,[135] in a remarkable display of scholarship, controverts Owen argument by argument. It is not possible here to take sides on this issue of the placing of the *Timaeus;* the problem is immensely complex, for every kind of scholarly and philosophic consideration has a bearing on it. Suffice it to say that the account just given of the *Parmenides* lends some backing to the thesis that the *Timaeus* should be counted among the middle dialogues,

---

132. *Timaeus* 52a4–5.

133. See David Ross, *Plato's Theory of Ideas*, pp. 1–10, for a summary.

134. G. E. L. Owen, "The Place of the *Timaeus* in Plato's Dialogues," *Classical Quarterly,* n.s. 3 (1953); reprinted in Allen, *Studies in Plato's Metaphysics.*

135. "Relation of the *Timaeus*," in Allen, *Studies in Plato's Metaphysics.*

while of course any independent argument supporting the earlier dating of the *Timaeus* constitutes a measure of support for the view of the *Parmenides* as a turning point.

According to a second alternative, the *Timaeus* exemplifies a reversion, on the part of Plato, to an earlier view; the dialogue is a symptom of a relapse, so to speak. In this view, Plato must be regarded as seeing, as he was writing the *Parmenides,* the problems by which his paradigm-forms are beset and as evolving a sparser and more analytical conception of forms which he then put to work in a number of later dialogues. Yet when in old age he turned to the philosophy of nature, to cosmology, he must, according to this view, be regarded as returning to a theory of forms which had been associated with the more metaphysical issues of some of the middle dialogues. It is hard to see how one would cite evidence either for or against this view, although the fact that this hypothesis requires us to attribute to Plato less philosophical self-awareness than tends to be characteristic of him perhaps deserves to be looked upon as counting against the conjecture of a relapse.

The third hypothesis, too, is no more than a "likely story."[136] Plato came to realize, as I have maintained, that the forms of his middle dialogues are required to perform two kinds of tasks that could not be carried out by one and the same entity. But according to this more attractive tale, Plato at the same time continued to seek solutions to both the logical and metaphysical problems for the sake of which these forms had been conceived. To that end, Plato develops distinct conceptions of forms for *both* of these functions, so that the enterprise of the *Parmenides* is not so much purging as it is separating or sorting out. At the same time, the *Phaedrus*—with its two modes of speech, the poetic and prosaic, and with forms that are objects both of vision and of analysis—can then be regarded as containing sketches of both types of forms, side by side.

---

136. *Timaeus* 29d2.

One conception of forms is subsequently utilized in the late "analytic" dialogues as the object of a dialectic that is understood to be collection and division, while forms as exemplars are utilized in the cosmology of the *Timaeus*.

Thus Plato, according to this third hypothesis, is more interested in philosophizing than in having a philosophy. Two hypotheses are tested in the effort to solve two clusters of problems and, in all likelihood, Plato was both aware of the tension between the proffered solutions and hopeful of a reconciliation. Without impatience, he refrains from a final commitment and eschews converting reflections into doctrines. Plato's awareness of the complexity of philosophy neither stunned him into silence nor impelled him to seek refuge in some comfortable dogma. Perhaps more than anything else, it is this openness which explains the fact that we may count among Platonists a Plotinus and a Galileo, a St. Bonaventure and a Bertrand Russell.

Index*

*No attempt was made to provide entries either for Plato or for Socrates.

203